Guidelines for Improving the Effectiveness of Boards of Directors of Nonprofit Organizations

Dr. Vic Murray

School of Public Administration
Faculty of Human and Social Development
University of Victoria

Dr. Yvonne Harrison

Department of Public Administration and Policy
Rockefeller College of Public Affairs and Policy
University at Albany, SUNY

Open SUNY Textbooks
2014

About the Textbook

The purpose of this book is to help boards of directors of nonprofit organizations improve their performance after completing the Board Check-Up, online board performance self-assessment tool found at www.boardcheckup.com.

It is important to understand, however, that this book can also be used as a stand-alone resource for any board seeking to assess its performance in that it contains the diagnostic questions on which the online self-assessment tool is based. It goes further by providing a framework for boards to use in discussing needed changes in board performance.

It also forms an integral part of a University at Albany, SUNY online course titled, *The Governance of Nonprofit Organizations*. This massive open online course (MOOC) can be taken for free or academic credit through Coursera's online teaching and learning platform.

For more information about this book, the Board Check-Up, and the nonprofit governance MOOC, please contact Prof. Yvonne Harrison at yharrison@albany.edu.

About the Authors

For the past dozen years, Vic Murray and Yvonne Harrison have worked collaboratively combining their knowledge and expertise to make research, education, and tools available to leaders in the nonprofit sector in need of them.

Vic Murray, Ph.D.

Vic Murray is currently Adjunct Professor in the School of Public Administration at the University of Victoria. From 1983 to 1995, he was director of the program in voluntary sector management in the Schulich School of Business at York University, Toronto.

Dr. Murray specializes in the study of voluntary sector organizations of all types with particular emphasis on the areas of board governance, strategic planning, inter-organizational collaboration, and the assessment of organizational effectiveness. He is also an active consultant and volunteer in these areas.

As Director of the Nonprofit Leadership and Management Program at York University he developed Canada's first certificate and master's level programs in that field. He is the author of many books, articles and papers in the fields of organizational behavior and nonprofit management. His most recent book is *The Management of Nonprofit and Charitable Organizations in Canada* (LexisNexis, 2009).

Currently, he is a member of the Advisory Board for the journal Nonprofit Management and Leadership, and active in the Association for Research on Nonprofit Organizations and Voluntary Action (ARNOVA). In 2002 he was awarded ARNOVA's Distinguished Lifetime Achievement Award. In 1995 the Canadian Centre for Philanthropy awarded him the Alan Arlett medal for distinguished contributions to philanthropy research.

In 2005, he helped to found the Association for Nonprofit and Social Economy Research of Canada and, in 2013, was awarded its Distinguished Service Award.

Dr. Murray's current research interest is a longitudinal study of the impact of the self-assessment of governance performance in nonprofit organizations (see www.boardcheckup.com) with Dr. Yvonne Harrison of the State University of New York at Albany.

Yvonne D. Harrison, Ph.D.

Yvonne Harrison is Assistant Professor in the Department of Public Administration and Policy in Rockefeller College of Public Affairs and Policy, University at Albany, SUNY. Prior to joining the Rockefeller College faculty, Yvonne was Assistant Professor in the Center for Nonprofit and Social Enterprise Management at Seattle University, Washington where she conducted nonprofit leadership research and taught courses in nonprofit governance and information management in nonprofit and government organizations.

Dr. Harrison has expertise in the governance and leadership of nonprofit organizations and the adoption and impact of information and communications technology (ICT) in nonprofit and voluntary sector organizations. Her current research examines questions about the effectiveness of nonprofit governing boards and the impact of online board performance self-assessment on nonprofit governance and organizational effectiveness. Funding for this research comes from the following sources:

- Institute for Nonprofit Studies, Mount Royal University in Calgary, Alberta, Canada
- University at Albany Faculty Research Award Programs (A and B)
- Rockefeller College of Public Affairs and Policy, University at Albany, SUNY

Currently, she is a member of the Association for Research on Nonprofit Organizations and Voluntary Action (ARNOVA) and Association for Nonprofit and Social Economy Research of Canada (ANSER).

In 2002, Dr. Harrison was awarded (with John Langford), the J. E. Hodgetts Award for Best Article in Canadian Public Administration (CPA). She is the author of a number of other peer reviewed journal articles, book chapters, research reports, and publications. She holds a Bachelor of Science in Nursing, a Master of Public Administration and PhD in Public Administration from the University of Victoria, British Columbia, Canada.

Reviewer's Notes

Review by Mike Flinton

Dr. Vic Murray and Dr. Yvonne Harrison have created a truly unique "how-to manual" that surpasses that clichéd label and successfully developed a management and leadership tool designed to help nonprofit board members, their CEOs, and aspiring nonprofit professionals to lead in an effective and efficient manner that insures participation by all.

This book is suitable for current board members and CEOs of nonprofit organizations in the U.S., Canada, or abroad, as well as graduate level faculty and students in the U.S. or Canada. Still others may find it helpful depending on the legal, social, and cultural environments that they and their nonprofit organizations operate in.

Having worked as a team, and by engaging hundreds of veteran board members and their organizations, Murray and Harrison use what they refer to as a "health check-up" assessment model and methodology. Using this, they've created a paradigm shift that enables nonprofit leaders to identify and explore the "Symptoms," "Diagnosis," and "Treatment" of the illnesses most common to nonprofit organizations. Throughout the 11 chapters of this guidebook, the authors remain committed to the health check-up analogy and process, which enables those in the trenches of nonprofit organizations, as well as those in the classroom, to use the text as a highly functional analysis and remedy tool.

Going well beyond a simple "how-to" mindset, the Symptoms, Diagnosis, and Treatment discussions on each topic are backed up with additional information accompanied by a plethora of .org, .com, .edu, and .gov web sites and print materials supporting what these two respected educators have to offer.

This publication can serve either as a standalone textbook or a supporting tool to the online Board Check-Up, which the authors developed before writing the guidebook. Hence, www.boardcheckup.com and the textbook were wisely developed for a variety of purposes and audiences.

Whether using it as an individual tool, or accompanying the self-assessment online through Board Check-Up, whether you are directly faced with the challenges of overseeing a nonprofit organization, responsible for teaching others "how to," or seeking to someday be a nonprofit professional yourself, you would be wise to examine this guidebook.

Mike Flinton has over 20 years experience as a not-for-profit and higher education professional. In addition to having served as the director of the Saratoga Automobile Museum in Saratoga Springs, NY he has enjoyed being a board member and leader in a variety of organizations ranging from the Executive Service Corps of the Tri-Cities (ESCOT) to the Underground Railroad History Project of the Capital Region among many others.

Before retiring from SUNY, Mike taught not-for-profit administration and management at SUNY Oneonta's nationally recognized Cooperstown Graduate Program in Museum Studies. He has also worked at four other SUNY campuses and mentored students from Skidmore College pursuing careers in the not-for-profit sector. He has advised and supported such widely recognized organizations as the Schenectady Museum (now called MiSci), Capital District Habitat for Humanity, Historical Albany Foundation, the World Awareness Children's Museum in Glens Falls, and Wiawaka Holiday House, a women's retreat center in Lake George. He is a regular guest lecturer at graduate level not-for-profit administration and management classes at UAlbany.

Before becoming a museum professional and consultant, Mike had a successful career in the United States Air Force where he lived and worked in more than a dozen countries and became involved in diverse social and public services programs, as well as history, art and cultural organizations in the U.S. and abroad.

Mike has an MS degree in Public Administration from Central Michigan University, an MA in History from University at Alabany SUNY, a BS in Business Management & Administration from University of Maryland's European Division and a BS in Human Resource Management from the New School of Social Research in New York City.

Review by Hélène Cameron

Guidelines for Improving the Effectiveness of Boards of Directors of Nonprofit Organizations will interest those who care about the governance of NPOs, especially board members, managers, and students of nonprofit organizations. The authors, Dr. Vic Murray and Dr. Yvonne Harrison, are specialists in the study of voluntary sector organizations and their deep understanding of the subject matter shows. As a practitioner with many years of experience with and on boards of nonprofit organizations, I have lived much of what is described in these guidelines. Murray and Harrison's comprehensive yet concise and accessible treatment of what makes boards tick is dead-on. They use an effective device patterned on the health check-up to link the "symptoms" of poor board performance with a "diagnosis" and "treatment" and recommend resources to consult for a deeper understanding and practical tools. It's all in one place... and it is readable and credible.

The guidebook mirrors Board Check-Up, an online self-assessment tool they designed to assist in improving board performance. Each chapter deals with one of the nine effectiveness challenges faced by the board: authority and responsibilities; role in planning, performance assessment, and fundraising; structure and operating procedures, including meetings; composition and development; informal culture; and finally, leadership.

Whether used in conjunction with the online tool or not, the guidebook should prove useful in several ways:

- as a framework for understanding the role, structure and operation of a board within a nonprofit organization
- as the basis for orienting novice board members to the nature and scope of their new environment
- in identifying the action that boards might take to improve performance and the resources and tools available to assist them
- in setting priorities for corrective action, based on an understanding of the potential impact of the assessed area and the feasibility of the remedy.

As the authors repeatedly counsel, boards have to do their own homework and find their own fit. This guidebook should help get the job done.

Through employment and community service, Hélène Cameron has an extensive background in non-profit governance, primarily in the areas of education and health. She gained valuable experience as the former executive director of non-profit organizations and as a volunteer and director on several non-profit boards in British Columbia. As a consultant, she has assisted several societies in the governance and strategic renewal process.

About Open SUNY Textbooks

Open SUNY Textbooks is an open access textbook publishing initiative established by State University of New York libraries and supported by SUNY Innovative Instruction Technology Grants. This pilot initiative publishes high-quality, cost-effective course resources by engaging faculty as authors and peer-reviewers, and libraries as publishing service and infrastructure.

The pilot launched in 2012, providing an editorial framework and service to authors, students and faculty, and establishing a community of practice among libraries.

Participating libraries in the 2012-2013 pilot include SUNY Geneseo, College at Brockport, College of Environmental Science and Forestry, SUNY Fredonia, Upstate Medical University, and University at Buffalo, with support from other SUNY libraries and SUNY Press. The 2013-2014 pilot will add more titles in 2015, and includes new participating libraries: SUNY Oswego, Monroe Community College, and more soon.

Contents

Acknowledgments

A special thanks to Chancellor Nancy Zimpher of the State University of New York and her staff for creating a strategy and source of funding to situate and advance our work. The following grants and people behind them deserve acknowledgement:

- 2014 Open SUNY Textbook Grant (Principal Investigators, Cyril Oberlander, Kate Pitcher, and Allison Brown);
- 2014 Open SUNY Innovative Instructional Technology Grant (IITG) (SUNY Open Director, Lisa Stephens); and
- 2014 University at Albany Online Teaching and Learning Grant (University at Albany Provost, Susan Phillips and Associate Provost for OTLG, Peter Shea).

These grants will begin the process of increasing access to nonprofit management and leadership education particularly students preparing for careers in the nonprofit sector and those working in the sector who face educational barriers such as cost and time constraints.

Finally, the web resources described in this book would not be possible without the research assistance and dedication of Sreyashi Chakravarty, a University at Albany, SUNY graduate student.

Chapter 1

Introduction

The purpose of this book is to help boards of directors of nonprofit organizations improve their performance after completing the online board self-assessment tool found at www. boardcheckup.com. However, it can also be used as a stand-alone resource for any board seeking to enhance its effectiveness in that it contains the diagnostic questions on which the online tool is based.

The approach taken here is similar to that which lies behind health checkups for individuals. Doctors usually begin by asking us to review a lengthy list of possible health issues and we check those about which we have concerns. The doctor and patient then focus their discussions on these issues. The typical process proceeds through the following three stages:

1. Understanding the *symptoms*. The doctor and patient begin by trying to define the issues more clearly.
2. *Diagnosis*. Effort is made to understand the *causes* of the problems through tests and further examinations.
3. *Treatment*. Once the problem has been properly diagnosed, a treatment program to remedy it is begun.

While the *Board Check-Up* survey on which this book is based does not claim to be as scientifically rigorous as a medical examination, it *is* based on the same logic. It begins by having those who belong to, or relate to, boards provide their perceptions of how well the board is working by guiding them through a list of potential "health issues," i.e. statements of possible problems, issues, or challenges that boards might encounter in their work. These statements have been derived from comments made by those who serve on boards or interact with them as well as from the work of researchers and consultants who have studied boards over the past 30 years. The process reveals both the things that the respondents feel the board is doing well in addition to those that are seen as problematic. Once issues (symptoms) have been identified, they become the focal point for discussions that explore how serious they are, what might be causing them (diagnosis), and what can be done to resolve them (treatment).

The Theory Behind the Guidelines

The conceptual framework on which the Board Check-Up is based is shown in Figure 1 below. It shows that effectiveness challenges faced by boards can be grouped in two dimensions: (a) the board's roles and responsibilities as a governing body; and (b) the factors that influence how well the board carries them out. Figure 1 further shows that within these two dimensions there exist nine basic sets of board effectiveness challenges. They are,

A. Effectiveness challenges related to the performance of the board's roles and responsibilities in the governance process.

1. The clarity of the board's role vis a vis management and other stakeholders in the organization's environment;

2. How well it carries out its duty to establish the organization's mission and the broad guiding strategic plans, priorities and general policies within which the organization should operate;

3. How clear and effective it is in carrying out its fiduciary role in assessing the performance of the organization and those to whom it delegates authority (e.g. the Chief Executive Officer) as well as its assessment of risks facing the organization.

4. How well it contributes to ensuring that the organization has the financial resources it needs to operate and achieve its mission.

B. Effectiveness challenges related to the factors that influence the board's ability to carry out its roles and responsibilities.

5. Aspects of the formal structure and operating procedures of the board such as its size, by-laws, job descriptions, committee structure, information systems, and administrative support;

6. The effectiveness of board meetings;

7. Various aspects of the makeup of the board's membership and how well board members are oriented and trained;

8. The role played by informal, shared attitudes and beliefs about how the board should behave, commonly known as the board's "culture";

9. The influence of two key people who provide formal and informal leadership to the board—the board Chair and the organization's top paid manager or CEO, if there is one.

Figure 1 recognizes that, taken together, these nine effectiveness challenges influence the performance of the organization as a whole (e.g. advancement of the mission, financial condition, efficiency, ability to learn and grow, motivation of paid staff and volunteers, and the support provided by stakeholders in the external environment).

It should be noted that boards are not the only contributors to the effectiveness of the organization.

Figure 1 shows the host of contextual factors that influence the governance process and the organization's effectiveness. Though they may often not be aware of it, a board's behavior may be affected by characteristics of the organization it governs—for example its history, size, and the nature of its mission. The actions of external stakeholders such as funders, regulators, and other organizations in the community or industry of which they are a part are also significant. Some of them have actual legal authority over some aspects of board responsibility while others have informal, yet powerful, forms of influence. Finally, all nonprofit organizations exist within a larger society. Countries and communities can differ widely in the political and economic climates they create. Cultural values about the nature of charity, volunteering and the role of nonprofits create different environments for the NPO's within them (see Salamon and Anheier, 1997).

For the purposes of this book we will not enter into in-depth discussions of these contextual influences on governance effectiveness. However, it must be noted that these influences are included in the Board Check-Up survey and are a focus of the larger research study of which the survey is a part. Papers produced from this research are available to registered users of the Board Check-Up (www.boardcheckup.com). Because the focus of this book is primarily practical, it will deal with the issues that challenge boards (symptoms), why they occur (diagnosis) and the ways that boards can consciously choose to improve their effectiveness in the governance process (treatment). Those interested in the growing body of academic research on the topic of contextual influences should see the 2014 Routledge Press book, *Innovative Perspectives in Nonprofit Governance*, edited by Chris Cornforth and Will Brown.

NINE ELEMENTS OF BOARD EFFECTIVENESS: A CONCEPTUAL FRAMEWORK

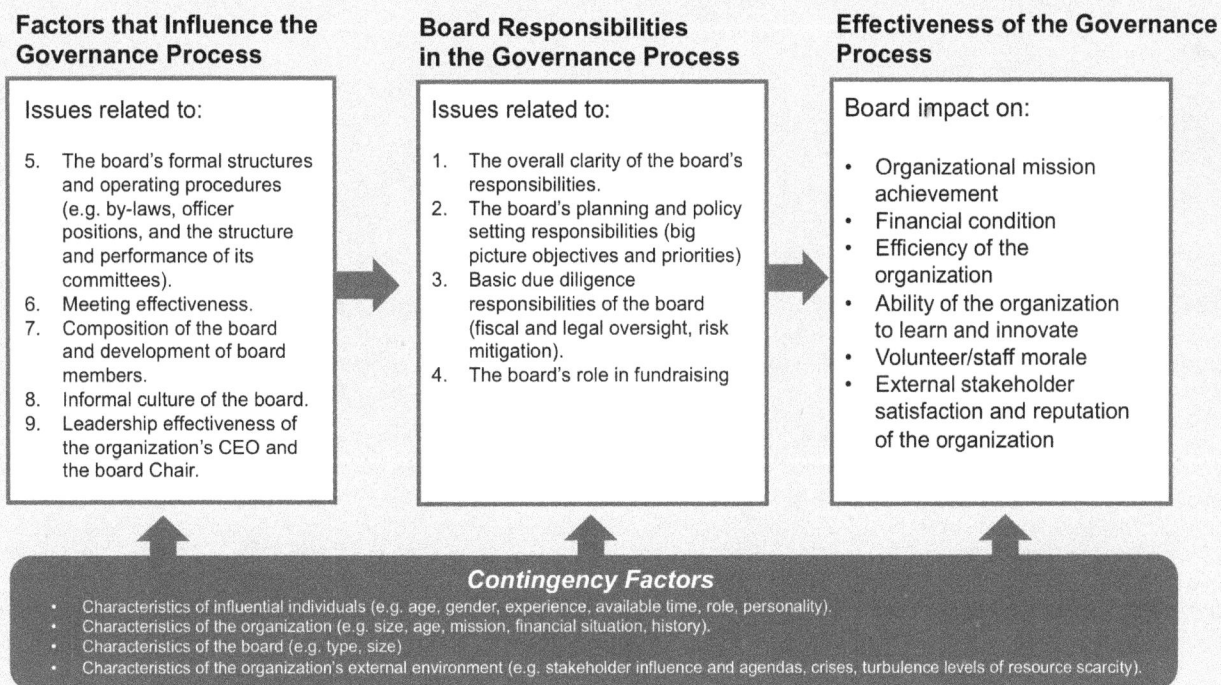

Factors that Influence the Governance Process

Issues related to:

5. The board's formal structures and operating procedures (e.g. by-laws, officer positions, and the structure and performance of its committees).
6. Meeting effectiveness.
7. Composition of the board and development of board members.
8. Informal culture of the board.
9. Leadership effectiveness of the organization's CEO and the board Chair.

Board Responsibilities in the Governance Process

Issues related to:

1. The overall clarity of the board's responsibilities.
2. The board's planning and policy setting responsibilities (big picture objectives and priorities)
3. Basic due diligence responsibilities of the board (fiscal and legal oversight, risk mitigation).
4. The board's role in fundraising

Effectiveness of the Governance Process

Board impact on:

- Organizational mission achievement
- Financial condition
- Efficiency of the organization
- Ability of the organization to learn and innovate
- Volunteer/staff morale
- External stakeholder satisfaction and reputation of the organization

Contingency Factors
- Characteristics of influential individuals (e.g. age, gender, experience, available time, role, personality).
- Characteristics of the organization (e.g. size, age, mission, financial situation, history).
- Characteristics of the board (e.g. type, size)
- Characteristics of the organization's external environment (e.g. stakeholder influence and agendas, crises, turbulence levels of resource scarcity).

Figure 1

Nine Elements of Board Effectiveness

Organization of this Book

As noted above, this book is intended to help boards assess their own performance and make decisions to improve the effectiveness of the governance process. Each chapter focuses on one of the nine dimensions of governance effectiveness described in Figure 1. The chapter starts with items relating to that dimension on the Board Performance Self-Assessment Questionnaire. These items represent the *symptoms* that indicate possible issues, problems, or challenges faced by the board. This is followed by a discussion of possible reasons that such symptoms might exist (diagnosis). The third part of each chapter looks at what might be done to alleviate the symptoms once a diagnosis is made (treatment). Included in this final part of the chapter are references to websites, books, and articles that provide additional advice and assistance on how to deal with the issues raised.

Chapter 2

The Board's Role and Responsibilities

Symptoms

While virtually everyone agrees that the role of the board in nonprofit organizations is to enable them to achieve their mission, differences arise when it comes to specifying *exactly* what the board's authority and responsibilities should be. In fact, this is probably the most frequently written about topic in the literature on nonprofit organization boards. Since most nonprofits also have paid or volunteer CEOs and managers, the question arises: what should the board's role and authority be compared to that held by these other important positions?

A high percentage of agreement with the following statements indicates that there is a lack of clarity in and around the board as to what its role ought to be:

☐ The board seems to be unclear about what its role ought to be.

☐ The board and the CEO or Executive Director sometimes seem to have different ideas about the authority each should have.

☐ The board tends to act too much as a "rubber stamp" for decisions made by the organization's top management.

☐ The board gets too involved in making decisions about operational details that ought to be made by management.

☐ Board members are unclear about their legal liabilities and what protection they have against them.

A closer look at the above statements shows there are actually two basic issues involved here:

1. What is the board's legal authority? There are certain duties boards *must* perform because they are legally responsible for the actions of the organization (as defined by those who authorize the organization to exist or give it tax exempt status). Their primary role is that of a fiduciary, which is to say that they are entrusted to look after the interests of the organization. In practical terms this translates into making

sure that the organization is achieving its mission, not wasting its money and not breaking any laws.

2. However, it is usually not feasible for boards to make *all* the decisions. While retaining responsibility for the overall performance of the organization, the board must delegate authority to others such as the CEO. (If it is an all-volunteer organization with no paid CEO, it may still delegate authority to volunteer committees or office holders). Those to whom authority is delegated have the power to make certain decisions, which the board can review only in the context of assessing the organization's overall performance. The question is, therefore, what matters should boards decide on and what should they delegate? This question is discussed under "Treatment" below.

Diagnosis

Why do boards and those who relate to them become confused about the authority of the board?

Regarding the board's legal authority, a lack of clarity usually exists because board members are not properly informed about the laws defining that authority and legal liability with respect to board activities. Confusion and lack of clarity about the board's responsibilities and decision-making authority arises for a number of reasons.

- The most common cause is that boards fail to adapt to changes in the organization's environment. Many nonprofit organizations start with very little money and few or no paid staff. As a result, volunteers conduct much of the work, and among the most active volunteers are board members. Meetings of boards often deal with everyday operating problems and small crises. When these organizations become more successful and are able to employ professional managers, many board members experience great difficulty in letting go of their involvement in day-to-day operations. At the same time the management team becomes frustrated over not knowing what they can decide and what they must refer to the board for decision. Once patterns of decision-making become established they form part of the board's informal culture and thus recede into the background to the point that they are taken for granted and never questioned.
- The same kind of confusion can arise when an organization experiences sudden major crises such as large funding cuts or unanticipated resignations of key staff. At such times boards often find themselves pushed into making operating decisions and don't know how or when to relinquish this role.
- In some cases, the lack of clarity exists because the CEO and key board members simply differ in their opinions about what the role of each party should be. If these root philosophical differences are never addressed directly, this situation leads to an endless series of disagreements over many issues.

Treatment

Lack of Clarity about the Board's Legal Authority and Liability

The basic knowledge about the board's legal authority and responsibility can be most easily obtained from a few good websites or written publications. These also provide important information about the nature and extent of a board's legal liabilities—the grounds on which boards can be sued for failure to carry out their duties properly. Normally, providing board members with orientation and simple written materials on this subject will suffice; however, if specific circumstances suggest that the organization faces any unusual situations, lawyers with specialized knowledge of this field should be consulted. It is important to realize that the laws on the duties and responsibilities of boards and their legal liability can vary from country to country and, in federated countries such as the U.S. and Canada, from one state or province to another.

Clarifying the Board's Role in Decision-making

The only way to deal with confusion or conflict around the role of the board is through education and discussion among all affected parties. This includes all board members, the board Chair, the organization's CEO, and other members of the management team who have expectations about the board carrying out certain actions. It should also include key funders or stakeholders who might feel they have some kind of authority to make decisions involving the organization.

Basic board responsibilities

To clarify the board's role, all those involved must understand the basic board responsibilities. These are described below. This material is adapted from Murray (2009).

To deal with the problem of achieving clarity regarding board roles and responsibilities, we need an understanding of what it is that boards do. The most common areas of responsibility in which boards may become involved are:

1. *Mission, values, goals, strategic priorities and performance assessment.* Setting the overall purpose for the organization—why it should exist, who it should serve, what services it should provide, and what values and ethical guidelines it should follow in providing them. This area also includes the setting of objectives and the development of broad strategic plans for achieving them. To do this properly requires assessing how well the organization has performed in achieving the goals set for it as well as understanding the challenges and opportunities that lie ahead.

2. *Fiscal/legal oversight and risk assessment.* Ensuring that the organization behaves in a fiscally and legally responsible manner. This includes such matters as overseeing operating and capital budgets, investments, property management and compliance with various laws applying to the organization. It also includes risk assessment—attempting to identify areas in which the organization is subjected to high risk to its assets or reputation.

3. *CEO selection and evaluation.* Ensuring that the best person holds the position of CEO and performs it at a satisfactory level of competence.

4. *Community relations* (also known as "Boundary Spanning"):
   - Representing the interests of the organization to its external publics;
   - Building alliances and partnerships with others that benefit the community; and
   - Ensuring that the interests of key external stakeholders are made known inside the organization.

5. *Resource development.* Ensuring that the organization obtains adequate funds to enable it to achieve its objectives.

6. *Management systems.* Ensuring that the organization is managed efficiently and effectively, e.g., that it has the right administrative structures and policies, information systems, human resources policies, etc.

7. *Board self-management.* Activities aimed at ensuring the board itself is as effective as it can be, e.g., recruiting, selecting and training its members, evaluating the effectiveness of its meetings and committees.

Roles of board members

To list the areas in which boards should have some kind of involvement is important, but it does not indicate *how* they should be involved. This is the question of the *roles* the board can play in the organization. It is common in writing about boards to talk only about the role of members as *decision-makers*. In addition, however, they may play two other critical roles: *advisor* and *implementer.* Thus there are at least three roles for board members:

1. *Decision-maker/evaluator.* The most important thing to understand about the decision-making role of the board is the concept of delegation. Except in the smallest of NPOs, the board cannot make all the decisions needed to get things done. It must trust staff and volunteers to make many decisions that it will never hear about. When the organization employs a CEO, the authority to make many decisions is delegated to that position and the CEO may, in turn, delegate some of that authority to others. The only decision the board makes about all these delegated matters is whether they all add up to satisfactory performance for the organization as a whole. This is the evaluation function of boards and it cannot be delegated. When the board *does* make decisions, it usually occurs only at the level of the whole board meeting in a formal session in which it votes on motions put forward to it.

2. *Advisor.* In this role, board members provide information and expert advice to their board and, less formally, to others such as the CEO or other management and staff. This role is usually played at the level of board committees, which may develop recommendations for the whole board or CEO. Individual members typically derive the information and advice they provide from the following sources:
   - Knowledge gleaned through their training and experience; and
   - Contacts in their networks. This latter contribution—the result of board members interacting with the outside world—has only recently been recognized as a vital part of the board's overall potential contribution (Renz, 2006; 2012)

3. *Implementer.* In a few instances, board members may actually carry out the activities required by the decisions they (or others) make. For example, they usually carry out the work of selecting future board members and selecting the CEO. They may also approach prospective donors for funds; participate in advocacy and community outreach efforts; or represent the organization in dealings with critical stakeholder groups. Implementation activities are usually carried out at the level of task forces or committees charged with specific governance functions such as fundraising or board recruitment. Occasionally, individual board members may get involved in implementing decisions such as approaching prospective donors to ask for contributions or presenting briefs on behalf of the organization to government bodies.

Patterns of Board Responsibility and When They are Appropriate

Understanding the kind of matters boards might get involved in and the various roles members can play is the first step to achieving clarity about what the board should do. However, the temptation is then to assume that there is a single pattern of board responsibilities and roles that is best for *all* NPOs. In spite of the assertions by some "how to do it" writers on boards that there is a "one best way" for all types of boards and governance situations, the limited research on what makes for an effective board suggests that there is not. Let us look at several models or common patterns of board roles and responsibilities and discuss when each may be appropriate.

The working board

There are conditions when it is quite acceptable to have board members who simultaneously participate in setting strategic directions, manage the implementation of plans and actually carry out "the work." The term for a board like this is the *working board*. A successful working board can exist when the nonprofit organization is new, small, or made up of all (or nearly all) volunteers and offers services that are not numerous or complex. For example, many self-help groups, small grassroots advocacy organizations, housing and food co-operatives, collectives, and sport organizations operate very successfully with working boards (Gill, 2005).

In working boards, board members are often the most committed and knowledgeable members of the organization and have worked up to the board as volunteers or were founders of the organization. It is not surprising, therefore, that some of them bring operational concerns to board meetings. In fact, in this model of board, it may be impossible to differentiate between "strategic" and "operational" leadership issues. For example, one botched special event fundraiser or bad story about a mishandled client in the newspaper could end the organization's existence. Almost anything and everything has the potential to be a "strategic" leadership issue. Getting established requires that the people involved are competent and have the energy to successfully wear many hats.

All that is needed to create an effective working board is to make sure that everybody is clear about who can make which decisions and who is going to do what. There should also be basic agreement about what things are the most important (priorities). In general, *whole-board meetings* of working boards should still focus on governance issues—planning for the future, setting broad objectives, setting priorities and assessing performance. But time at board meetings spent on apparent "details" is not necessarily wasted *if* the chair or others can spot the larger strategic issues that can be buried in them. In these kinds of small organizations the board can benefit by holding periodic special meetings of all active participants (such as other key volunteers and any staff) to discuss "how well are we doing in fulfilling our mission?," and "where do we go from here?"

The working board is *not* appropriate under conditions opposite to those that fit it best, that is, organizations with paid staff and full-time managerial personnel who are operating programs competently. Most public institutions such as universities, hospitals and mid to large sized social service agencies are examples of the kinds of organizations that fit these conditions. Such organizations cannot tolerate the confusion created by board members trying to "micro manage" the organization's affairs when others are better prepared to do so.

The governance-only board

A *governance-only board* is one that restricts itself to providing broad, strategic leadership (Gill, 2005) to the organization by focusing primarily on issues that relate to the basic strategic question of "who is to receive what services at what cost" (Carver, 2006). This means that decision-making/evaluating becomes the key role being played by the board.

The dilemma facing the large, complex institutions for whom governance-only boards are the most appropriate, and one of the reasons they can so easily become rubber-stamp boards, is that most board members are busy civic leaders who, though great supporters of the organization, have very little time to become thoroughly knowledgeable about it or the sector in which it operates (such as healthcare, education, or the arts). This makes informed debate about major strategic issues very difficult. For example, it takes a lot of expertise to know whether an organization should merge with another (or cease to exist), whether a university should open (or close) a department or whether a hospital should convert a certain percentage of its beds from active to chronic care.

The secret of creating an effective governance-only board lies in developing a shared understanding of basic levels of policy, deciding which of them are basic "strategic" or "landmark" governance issues and devising information systems that supply valid data on past performance and future needs in ways that clearly relate to them (see Chait et al, 2005 for a discussion of "landmark" governance issues).

The mixed model board

Many boards in practice are neither purely working boards nor governance-only boards. They tend to be located between the two ends of the board involvement continuum. Sometimes they may become very involved in making decisions about day-to-day operations while at other times they keep their involvement limited to matters of policy and strategy. In these organizations, paid managers may make most of the operating decisions but may not have the time or expertise to handle certain functions with which they are not familiar, for example, publicity, fundraising or government relations. In such situations it might be expedient to turn to board members for expertise and implementation assistance.

Other times that a governance-only board might revert to a mixed model state is during a major crisis such as the loss of large grants, financial mismanagement, serious labor unrest or the actions of militant client groups. Insofar as the paid manager has trouble handling these situations, the temptation on the part of the board to get involved in the direct management of them can be strong; indeed managers may ask for it and it may be necessary. Once the crisis is over, however, it is easy to allow things to continue in an inappropriate mixed model state rather than reverting to the prior governance-only model.

It *is* possible to sustain a mixed model form of governance that can work well. In this situation, certain board members or committees take responsibility for managing specific operational leadership functions. These would typically be seen as working committees and their chairs become de facto operating managers. At the level of the whole board, effort must still be made to focus primarily on strategic issues. Insofar as possible, the operational committees and board members with specific operational responsibilities should work under the authority of the Executive Director.

The mixed model is a difficult one to implement successfully because there are so many occasions where confusion can arise, especially as the organization's environment continues to change. The secret of success lies in exceptionally full and open communication in which all parties feel free to raise questions over gaps or overlaps in authority and responsibility. There must also be high levels of tolerance for ambiguity. For example, even though the primary purpose of meetings of the whole board should be for discussing major issues of policy and strategy, some board members will want to talk about matters pertaining to their responsibilities as operational managers. They may thus seem to be cluttering the meetings with "managerial" details and undermining the authority of the CEO. The key to success lies in training everybody—management and board alike—to recognize what is "strategic" and redirect the non-strategic matters to the CEO.

Summary

In summary, there is no "one best way" of structuring the roles and responsibilities of a board of directors that fits all situations. The board cannot avoid its legal requirement of exercising due diligence in ensuring that the organization achieves its mission, has a strategic plan and does not get into financial or legal difficulties. However, the way it gets involved in the other responsibility areas discussed above, can be highly variable. The important thing to understand is that the board is part of the whole organizational system that includes paid mangers, staff, volunteers, and external stakeholders. All have roles to play in the process of deciding what to do and then implementing those decisions. Everyone must be clear about who will do the deciding, who will have input into those decisions, who will do the implementing and what information will be obtained to assess how well the decisions have worked out.

Table 1 contains numerous links to useful information and resources to increase governance effectiveness in the area of the board's legal authority and fiduciary responsibilities.

Table 1

Additional resources on the board's legal authority and responsibilities

Topic	Country	Source Website
Legal Duties and Liabilities of Directors	U. S. A.	National Council of Nonprofits http://www.councilofnonprofits.org/resources/resources-topic/boards-governance/roles-and-responsibilities-nonprofit-boards
	Britain	Government of the United Kingdom http://www.charitycommission.gov.uk/detailed-guidance/trustees-staff-and-volunteers/the-essential-trustee-what-you-need-to-know-cc3/#i1
	Canada	Industry Canada https://www.ic.gc.ca/eic/site/cilp-pdci.nsf/eng/cl00693.html
		Carter's Law http://www.carters.ca/pub/article/charity/govset/A-duties.pdf
	Australia	Institute of Community Directors of Australia http://www.communitydirectors.com.au/icda/tools/?articleId=1362
Basic Board Responsibilities	U.S.A.	National Council of Nonprofits http://www.councilofnonprofits.org/resources/resources-topic/boards-governance/roles-and-responsibilities-nonprofit-boards
	Britain	Know How Nonprofit http://knowhownonprofit.org/leadership/governance/getting-started-in-governance/the-responsibilities-of-company-directors/?searchterm=board%20of%20directors%20responsibilities
	Australia	Our Community https://www.ourcommunity.com.au/boards/boards_article.jsp?articleId=1310

Chapter 3

The Board's Role in Planning

Symptoms

It is commonly accepted "best practice" that a major role for boards ought to be thinking about the "big picture" of how the organization is doing and where it ought to be heading in the future. It is usually recommended that this big picture thinking be captured in a "Strategic Plan" which can be used as a guide by all in the organization in making specific policy decisions. A high percentage of agreement with the following statements would indicate that the board might be having problems with its role in the planning function:

☐ The board has not spent enough time establishing a clear mission and vision for the organization.

☐ The board never seems to have time to explore external challenges and opportunities that the organization might face.

☐ The board does not do a very good job of learning about the concerns of external stakeholders who can influence the organization.

☐ The board does not do a very good job of learning about the concerns of the communities that the organization serves.

☐ The board rarely holds "creative thinking" sessions aimed at trying to find new ways the organization could develop.

☐ The board does little to learn about innovations tried by others that might help the organization.

☐ The board is not provided with a clear enough picture of the organization's internal strengths and limitations in dealing with its external environment.

☐ The board has not developed a clear, well-researched, strategic plan that sets out broad goals and establishes priorities for the organization.

☐ Plans exist on paper but they don't get implemented at the operational level, i.e. other concerns drive what actually gets done.

Diagnosis

The main reasons that boards have difficulties with fulfilling their planning function effectively are:

- The organization faces an external environment that is too turbulent or complex to understand hence the board feels it is not possible to make plans for the future. (Note, however, that it may be possible to develop useful scenarios based on several different hypothesized futures.)
- Lack of clarity about who should play what role in the planning process. Boards are often accused of "rubber-stamping" when they think their job is simply to approve the plans brought to them by management (Chait et al., 2005).
- Lack of understanding of the planning process. This can occur because the board does not contain enough members who have experience in strategic planning, or who have not been provided with the opportunity to learn about it.
- Lack of time. This is usually due to meeting agendas that are too full of "routine" matters or short-term "firefighting" issues that do not allow the board to step back and look at the big picture.
- Structural problems. The board has not created a committee whose function it is to engage in the in-depth information gathering and analysis that is necessary for effective strategic planning.

Treatment

To treat planning problems, consider the following points:

- Decide on the role in the planning process that is best for the board given the organization's unique characteristics (its age, size, presence of experienced senior managers, number of members with strategic planning experience, etc.). Choose between one of these three basic roles:
  - Doing it all themselves, i.e. the board obtains all needed information and decides on recommended directions;
  - Using a board committee with responsibilities for planning to work along with members of the management team in obtaining the needed information and creating the recommended directions;
  - Having the needed information and recommendations developed by the management team (with or without the help of consultants) and presented in draft form for the board to discuss and decide upon.
- Ensure that there is sufficient time, money, and expertise for those responsible for preparing the initial draft of the strategic plan to carry out that work.
- Provide education in strategic planning to all board members who lack sufficient experience (see below for a brief outline of what is involved in strategic planning).

Always involve the organization's CEO and other members of the management team in providing needed information on the state of the organization's external environment and internal capacity. *But,* also attempt to find reliable information from independent sources on these same matters. For example, many sub-sectors within the nonprofit world have evolved associations and professional bodies that monitor and report on opportunities and potential threats in the environment. There are also usually a number of experienced consultants in each industry of whom boards should be aware.

The next section provides an overview of strategic leadership questions within the basic elements of a strategic plan, from Murray (2014).

Overview of Key Questions Addressed in a Strategic Plan

1. Mission

What is the purpose of the organization? Why does it exist? Who does it serve?

2. Values

What values should the organization uphold in the process of doing its work? For example:
- What is the underlying philosophy behind its approach to the way it seeks to achieve its mission?
- What beliefs and attitudes should be shared regarding the way the organization wants to work with the public, its clients, volunteers, staff and other stakeholders?

3. Vision

Many strategic plans contain a statement describing a vision for the organization's future. A vision statement answers such questions as:
- What should the organization look like in 5 years?
- What will it be known for?
- What will it be doing that is different from what it does now?
- What will be its reputation among other organizations in the same field?

(Note: Many find it is better if this section is tackled after steps 4 and 5 below.)

4. The environmental context of the organization's operations

This is a very important section that outlines the challenges and opportunities that shape the reality within which the board must work. It addresses such questions as:
- What changes are likely to occur in the next 2-3 years in the following aspects of the external world and what implications will they have on the organization's operations:
  - The economy
  - The political environment
  - Societal values and beliefs
  - Technology
  - Demographics
- Who are the critical stakeholders who influence the ability of the organization to succeed? Examples of stakeholders include those the organization seeks to serve,

funders (and potential funders) of all types, regulators, potential allies and collaborators, key "competitors" for funds, or clients/audience.

For each of the key stakeholders answer these questions:

- What do they want from the organization, and how are these wants likely to change in the next 2-3 years? How much influence do they have over the organization's ability to carry out its mission?
- To what extent do their expectations of the organization conflict with one another?
- What are the organizations that are similar in size, mission, types of programs, etc. and what are they doing that the organization might learn from?

5. The internal capacity of the organization

What are the present internal strengths and weaknesses of the organization in terms of resources, people, administrative systems and leadership capabilities? In other words, what is the organization's *capacity* for influencing, or successfully adapting to, the external environment that it will likely be facing in the next few years?

6. Strategic goals and priorities

There is usually no way that any organization is able to find the time, money and people to do everything that it would like to do in an ideal world. So what should be the key strategic goals for the organization over the next two years in these major components of your operations?

(a) Programs
- Should there be any changes in the kind of people the organization serves?
- What changes are needed in the quantity and quality of the programs or services provided to those people?
- How many and what kind of *additional* programs (beyond those currently in place) are needed to support the mission?

(b) Resources
- What is the potential for increasing financial support from all sources to support programs priorities?
- What should be the organization's resource development goals and which of them are most feasible to implement?

(c) Capacity building
- What changes are needed in leadership development, staffing, volunteering, information technology and other management systems to support program and resource development priorities? Which of these changes are needed most?

7. Prioritization

Among the goals identified, which have the highest priority in terms of importance and urgency?

8. Implementation

Strategic plans are often ineffective because the goals and priorities they identify do not get translated into implementable operational plans for which individuals take responsibility. Are there connections between the strategic priorities and more detailed business plans and budgets? Are these connections obvious and strong?

9. Accountability

As well, ineffectiveness can result when results are not tracked or when there are no widely accepted systems in place for doing this. This can result in an outdated or obsolete plan. To avoid this, the organization's plan must contain agreed upon procedures for the assessment of progress and the plan must be reviewed and updated annually in the light of this assessment.

For additional guidelines on strategic planning and the board's role and capacity to engage in it, see the resources in Table 2.

Table 2

Additional Resources on the Board's Role in Planning

Topic	Country	Source Website
Board's Role in Strategic Planning	Britain	KnowHow NonProfit http://knowhownonprofit.org/funding/service/commercial-masterclasses/strategy-for-public-services-1/strategic-planning-and-how-does-it-involve-the-board
How to do Strategic Planning	U.S.A.	Free Management Library http://managementhelp.org/freenonprofittraining/strategic-planning.htm
		National Council of Nonprofits http://www.councilofnonprofits.org/strategic-business-planning-for-nonprofits
		Zimmerman Lehman Consulting http://www.zimmerman-lehman.com/strategic.htm
	Britain	KnowHow Nonprofits http://knowhownonprofit.org/organisation/strategy
	Australia	Institute of Community Directors of Australia https://www.ourcommunity.com.au/icda/tools/?articleId=1368

Topic	Country	Source Website
Evaluating Strategic Planning Outcomes	U.S.A.	Innovation Network http://www.innonet.org/?section_id=64&content_id=182

Chapter 4

The Board's Role in Performance Assessment

Symptoms

Boards of nonprofit organizations are required to exert due diligence in ensuring that the organizations they govern are achieving their missions effectively and efficiently. Quite aside from legal requirements, most boards feel an obligation to hold those who run the organization accountable for achieving results in carrying out the responsibilities delegated to them. They also wish to be able to identify and recognize what is being done well in the organization. In turn, boards are morally and legally accountable to those for whom they act as trustees. To fulfill all these accountability responsibilities requires that the board receive reliable and valid information on how things are going. The areas in which due diligence assessments need to be carried out are:

- The performance of the organization as a whole. This includes:
    - Attainment of strategic plan objectives.
    - Assurance of the organization's financial and legal soundness.
    - Assurance that the organization is aware of serious potential risks it may face and is mitigating them as well as possible.
    - Assurance that all members of the organization (including board members themselves) are behaving ethically and in accord with the espoused values of the organization, e.g. avoiding conflicts of interest, mistreatment of clients or staff, etc.
- The performance of the organization's CEO (paid or unpaid top management person).
    - Assurance that the CEO is meeting the performance expectations of the position.
- The performance of the board itself.
    - Assurance that the board is governing effectively and is meeting its own accountability objectives.

Indications that the board is experiencing challenges in this area of their responsibilities arise when a significant numbers of board members or others related to the board, such as the CEO, management team and other key stakeholders report high levels of agreement with the following statements:

☐ The board does not do a satisfactory job of assessing how well the organization is achieving its mission.

☐ The board does not get enough of the right kind of information to give it a clear picture of how well the organization is doing.

☐ The board does not ensure that an analysis is done of serious risks that the organization might face.

☐ The board does not do a very good job of ensuring that the organization's finances are being managed soundly.

☐ The board does not regularly and systematically carry out assessments of the CEO's performance (e.g. Executive Director, President, etc.).

Diagnosis

The main reasons for difficulties that boards may have in carrying out their duties in the critical area of performance assessment are as follows:

- There is lack of clarity about the amount and kind of assessments the board should undertake. Either the management and board have differing ideas about this, or the board itself is unsure what its role in performance assessment is.
- The board may *wish* to assess performance but it does not get sufficient information to enable it to carry it out. This could be because there are inadequate systems for gathering and reporting it (including metrics and frameworks to organize it) or because it is intentionally or unintentionally withheld from the board by the management team.
- The board does not create suitable internal structures and processes for carrying out its assessment duties, i.e. there are no board officers or committees with responsibility for gathering the needed performance data, analyzing it and bringing assessment results to the full board for proper consideration.
- The board is not adequately trained in performance management, or does not have enough members with knowledge of how to analyze and interpret performance data.
- The board has evolved an informal culture in which it believes that it does not have to take one or more of its performance assessment responsibilities seriously. For example, it may feel uncomfortable monitoring and evaluating the performance of the CEO or raising questions about the validity or amount of information it is given about the organization's finances or reputation in the community.

Treatment

Some of the general approaches to improving the board's ability to carry out its performance assessment responsibilities are as follows.

- The most important requirement is to develop a supportive culture for evaluation not only within the board but also in the whole organization. There must be an atmosphere of collaboration, trust and respect between the board, the top management team and, indeed, all those who control information on how well the organization is doing. If there is a feeling that information is going to be used by the board to 'blame' or punish somebody for doing a bad job, the process of assessment will turn into one of political game playing between the evaluators and those under evaluation. This is why boards must be willing and able to communicate positive evaluation results as much, or even more, than those that suggest problems.

- The next question, of course, is: How do you change a board's culture when most people are not even aware such a thing exists? This is where the leadership of the board chair and the organization's CEO becomes important. Boards are more likely to face the need to change aspects of their culture when those they respect lead them in examining their heretofore taken-for-granted assumptions about how they do things like performance assessment.

- It is also vital that board members receive *training and development* in performance management, including how to obtain and interpret the information provided in each of the key areas of assessment: strategic plan objectives, financial soundness, risk mitigation, CEO performance and the board's own performance.

- Finally, it is necessary to create structures within the board that facilitate carrying out its performance assessment responsibilities. This usually means creating committees or officer positions in which the duties include gathering, analyzing and making recommendations about performance in each of the areas identified above. Leaving such matters to the board as a whole, or delegating them to the CEO and management team, will usually result in less than effective oversight.

What follows is a discussion of resources that will help boards in each of the specific areas of performance assessment identified above.

Assessing the Performance of the Organization as a Whole

As mentioned above, the major problems with evaluation of organizational performance lie in the areas of choosing suitable effectiveness criteria, developing a framework to organize criteria, and choosing the best methods of measurement and analysis.

- For information on what constitutes nonprofit organizational effectiveness see Herman and Renz (2008). Herman and Renz advance "Nine theses" to explain nonprofit organizational effectiveness. For a discussion of the subjectivity inherent in assessing effectiveness and how to deal with it, see Murray (2010).

- For a conceptual framework for understanding organizational effectiveness criteria, see The *Competing Values Framework* (CVF) Quinn and Rohrbaugh (1981; 1983). The CVF depicts means and ends effectiveness criteria in two dimensions (structure and focus) drawn from the four schools of organizational thought (rational goal, internal process, human relations, and open systems). It has been useful as a diagnostic and leadership development tool at the individual and group levels (see Quinn, Faerman, Thompson, McGrath, & St. Clair (2010).

- For yet another framework to help boards conceptualize, organize, and measure performance, see Robert Kaplan and David Norton's (1996) Balanced Score Card. The BSC organizes measurements along different organizational perspectives (e.g. financial, internal operations, client/customer and learning and innovation). In a 2013 study titled *Board Member Self-Perception of Organizational Governance and the Role of the Balanced Score Card*, Aulgur found support for use of the BSC to help boards become clear about their role as well as overcome problems from social construction of organizational performance (i.e. what matters most). Others have found that it does not work as well in some types of nonprofit organizations (e.g. social service).

The Board's Role in Financial Management

As stewards of nonprofit organizations, one of the board's responsibilities is to ensure there are enough financial resources to advance the mission and work of the organization and that these resources are being spent wisely. Effective oversight in this area involves tracking the following aspects of financial management:

- Audits of past financial expenditures;
- Oversight of the adequacy of incoming financial resources and reserves (e.g. ensuring there is enough money to cover planned and unexpected expenditures); and
- Monitoring the annual budget.

Most boards are highly conscious of their responsibility for ensuring that their organization is managed in a financially responsible manner. But this is easier said than done, especially when many board members have little or no expertise in understanding financial statements, auditor's reports, budget documents and the concepts behind financial strategies. Nevertheless, it is possible for boards to improve their competency in this vital area by:

- Conducting regular reviews of board competency in understanding the financial condition of the organization and providing training in overcoming areas in need of improvement.
- Insisting that CEOs provide all relevant financial information needed to adequately understand the organization's finances.
- Obtaining independently generated reports on the organizations financial management, e.g. from auditors, industry associations, consultants, etc.

For research on the relationship between board effectiveness and nonprofit financial health see Hodge and Piccolo (2011). For guidance on financial management, Miller (2008) answers important financial questions, including the relationship between revenue sources and profitability. This article provides helpful information for boards considering financial decisions such as diversification of revenue streams as well as whether to fund new programs or not.

Risk Management

The concept of risk management in nonprofit organizations refers to becoming aware of actions or events which have the potential to harm the organization's reputation in the community, its financial stability, or cause it to incur legal liabilities. Examples include risks to client or employee health and safety, high-risk investments, actions that could be construed as negative by the public, etc. The aim of risk management is to balance the possible benefits derived from taking risks against their possible negative effects.

- Good advice and a sample conflict of interest policy can be found in Gill (2005).
- Jackson (2006) contains specific guidance along with useful tools and resources.

Assessing the Performance of the CEO

One of the most important decisions a board makes concerns the selection of the CEO. Much time and energy goes into preparing the job description, recruiting and selecting the right candidate, and orienting them to the top job. Equally important, however, is the need to assess how well CEOs are working out once they are in office. For more specific guidance on the topic of performance assessment, check out the websites in Table 3.

Table 3

Additional Performance Assessment Resources

Topic	Country	Source Website
Overall Assessment of Organizational Performance	U.S.A.	Free Management Library http://managementhelp.org/aboutfml/diagnostics.htm
		Fieldstone Alliance http://www.fieldstonealliance.org/client/articles/Tool-revenue_Evaluation_Matrix.cfm
		Innovation Network http://www.innonet.org/?section_id=64&content_id=185
		Harvard Family Research Project http://www.hfrp.org/evaluation/the-evaluation-exchange/issue-archive/democratic-evaluation
Assessment of Finances and Financial Management	U.S.A.	Free Management Library http://managementhelp.org/organizationalperformance/nonprofits/finances.htm
		The Bridgespan Group http://www.bridgespan.org/Publications-and-Tools/Nonprofit-Boards/Nonprofit-Boards-101/Fiduciary-Responsibilities-Board-Members.aspx#.U1E6DvldX-o
		The Greater Washington Society of CAs http://www.nonprofitaccountingbasics.org/reporting-operations/finance-committee-committee-chair-responsibilities
		National Council of Nonprofits http://www.councilofnonprofits.org/nonprofit-audit-guide/board-role-audit-committee

Topic	Country	Source Website
		CompassPoint http://www.compasspoint.org/sites/default/files/documents/Guide%20to%20Fiscal%20Policies%20and%20%20Procedures.pdf
		Washington Secretary of State http://www.sos.wa.gov/_assets/charities/What%20Board%20Members%20Need%20To%20Know%20(JJ).pdf
	Britain	KnowHow NonProfit http://knowhownonprofit.org/organisation/operations/financial-management/measuring
		http://knowhownonprofit.org/organisation/operations/financial-management/budgets
		http://knowhownonprofit.org/leadership/governance/getting-started-in-governance/financial-responsibilities-of-the-board
		Funding Central http://www.fundingcentral.org.uk/Page.aspx?SP=6240
	Canada	United Church of Canada http://www.united-church.ca/files/handbooks/financial.pdf
		Alberta Ministry of Culture and Community http://culture.alberta.ca/community-and-voluntary-services/programs-and-services/board-development/resources/workbooks/pdfs/Financial_Responsibilities09.pdf
		K.D. Wray, Consultants http://www.wrayca.com/?page_id=634
Assessment of Finances and Financial Management	Australia	Leadership Victoria http://www.leadershipvictoria.org/docs/skills-builder-fact-sheet_final.pdf
		CPA Australia http://www.cpaaustralia.com.au/~/media/Corporate/AllFiles/Document/professional-resources/auditing-assurance/guide-understanding-audit-assurance.pdf

Topic	Country	Source Website
The Role of the Board Finance Committee	U.S.A.	Greater Washington Society of CPAs http://www.nonprofitaccountingbasics.org/reporting-operations/budgeting-financial-planning
		National Council of Nonprofits http://www.councilofnonprofits.org/nonprofit-audit-guide/board-role-audit-committee
The Board's Role in Preventing Fraud	U.S.A.	Venables http://www.venable.com/preventing-and-investigating-fraud-embezzlement-and-charitable-asset-diversion-whats-a-nonprofit-board-to-do/
		Association of Certified Fraud Examiners http://acfe.gr/wp-content/uploads/2013/10/managing-business-risk.pdf
	U.S.A.	Keller and Owens http://www.kellerandowens.com/resources/FraudBooklet.pdf
	Australia	Council of Social Services of New South Wales http://www.itbusinessedge.com/slideshows/show.aspx?c=93089
The Board's Role in Managing Risk	U.S.A.	National Council on Nonprofits http://www.councilofnonprofits.org/resources/resources-topic/risk-management-and-insurance
		Public Counsel http://www.publiccounsel.org/tools/publications/files/risk_management.pdf
		Nonprofit Risk Management Center http://www.nonprofitrisk.org/library/articles/board120307.shtm
	Britain	KnowHow NonProfit http://knowhownonprofit.org/studyzone/how-to-carry-out-a-risk-assessment-1 http://knowhownonprofit.org/how-to/how-to-complete-a-risk-assessment
	Canada	Imagine Canada http://library.imaginecanada.ca/files/nonprofitscan/kdc-cdc/prince_albert_planning_guide.pdf

Topic	Country	Source Website
		Carter Law http://www.carters.ca/pub/checklst/nonprofit.pdf
	Australia	Our Community http://www.ourcommunity.com.au/management/view_help_sheet.do?articleid=1
Performance Evaluation of the CEO	U.S.A.	Free Management Library http://managementhelp.org/boards/evaluating-chief-executive.htm
		Compass Point http://www.compasspoint.org/board-cafe/annual-evaluation-executive-director

Chapter 5

The Board's Role in Fundraising

Symptoms

Effectively performing the board's role in fundraising is one of the most common challenges reported by both board members and those with whom they have relationships. Dissatisfaction in this area comes in three forms:

1. A lack of clarity about the board's role in fundraising relative to that of paid staff and/or professional fundraisers.
2. A feeling of dissatisfaction with the board's activities related to fundraising.
3. Individual board member reluctance or lack of knowledge about how to engage in fundraising.

High levels of agreement with the following statements indicate challenges in this area:

☐ The board seems confused about its role in fundraising for the organization.

☐ The board has not approved an overall strategy for fundraising.

☐ The board has problems engaging in actual fundraising activities.

Diagnosis

The main reasons for dissatisfaction with the board's role in fundraising are:

- Criteria used (formally or informally) in selecting board members do not include checking for a prospective recruit's willingness to help with fundraising or experience with this activity.
- Potential board nominees are not informed beforehand regarding expectations of board members in the fundraising area.
- Differing expectations exist between the board's understanding of what its role in fundraising should be and those held by the CEO and/or professional fundraising staff.
- Orientation and training of new board members does not include coverage of the board's role in fundraising.

- There is a lack of a clear overall fundraising strategy for the organization and/ or a clear structure indicating who is responsible for what in implementing the fundraising plan.
- There is lack of awareness of the range of roles and responsibilities that board members may play in fundraising.
- There is a lack of leadership within the board that helps members accept a more active role in fundraising activities.

Treatment

The first step in optimizing the board's contribution to the generation of financial resources for the organization is to understand the full range of roles and responsibilities it could undertake. Table 4 illustrates the potential board roles and responsibilities in fundraising.

Table 4

Board Roles and Responsibilities in Fundraising

Responsibilities	Roles		
	Board	**Committee**	**Individual Board Member**
Approve strategy developed by others	Definitely	Never	Never
Participate in developing strategy	Possibly	Usually	Possibly
Help implement strategy	Usually	Usually	Usually
Oversee implementation of strategy	Possibly	Usually	Possibly

It can be seen from Table 4 that there that there are three possible roles for board member involvement:

1. As part of the board acting as a whole in the same way it does during official board meetings.

2. As part of a special fundraising committee containing board members. *Note: It is important to understand that fundraising committees do not have to be committees of the board and, if they are, they can contain some members who are not board members. Such committees should normally only help develop plans and policies to recommend to others for approval or assist in actually implementing fundraising activities.*

3. As an individual acting alone, for example as one does when making a donation to the organization or visiting a potential donor.

Down the left hand side of Table 4, it can also be seen that there are four possible levels of responsibility that can be taken up by the board:

1. Responsibility for reviewing and approving fundraising strategies, plans and policies developed by others such as fundraising professionals, a fundraising committee, etc. This is usually done at official meetings of the board as a whole.

2. Becoming involved in the *creation* of fundraising strategies, plans and policies, often within a fundraising committee.

3. Once plans are in place, there is the hard work of actually raising the money—holding special events, soliciting corporate sponsorships, applying for grants, running mail campaigns, asking potential big donors for support or just giving fundraisers contacts to approach. Insofar as these tasks involve the board (as they might in the case of a working board for example), they would usually be carried out through a fundraising committee or by individual board members volunteering their time.

4. Finally, there is the job of developing systems for obtaining valid data on how effective fundraising activities are, tracking the results—receiving and reviewing reports and suggesting changes if needed. This responsibility is often the job of a board fundraising committee but could, in some circumstances, be carried out by the board as a whole.

It is important to understand that there is no "one best way" when it comes to the board's involvement in fundraising. The content in each of the boxes in Table 4 represents common practice and should not be taken as the way it *ought* to be in all cases. Each organization must decide for itself which responsibilities should be carried out by whom and at what level—that of the board as a whole, a committee or the individual board member. Where the board belongs on the fundraising involvement continuum depends greatly on a few factors:

- The ability of the organization to employ professional fundraisers. Such people are experts in developing plans and leading teams who will implement them. Small, new and low budget nonprofits can rarely afford this kind of support so the work has to be undertaken by volunteers and staff usually working in a committee structure. Board members can sit on committees and contribute as individuals.
- The level of commitment and experience/knowledge about fundraising among board members.
- The availability and expertise of other volunteers, external supporters and potential partners who could provide assistance in this area.

Once it is decided who should play what roles in doing what, the next job is making sure everyone is capable of performing those roles. In the case of fundraising, this can involve making the following changes:

- Developing criteria for the kind of person you want to recruit to your board so as to increase fundraising competency. If members will be expected to play a role other than general oversight, they should be ready and willing to do so. *Note: It is not necessary for all board members to be fundraising whizzes but, if you want involvement, some should be.*
- Provide training and development. Much of fundraising consists of learnable skills. Orientation and training for board members should address them.
- If the analysis of possible roles carried out in Table 4 reveals that a committee should be involved, be careful and thorough in defining its terms of reference so it does not tread on the toes of fundraising staff or take over the job of the board as a whole which is responsible for policy decisions made in this area of board responsibility.

For further information on the board's role in fundraising, see the useful websites in Table 5.

Table 5
Additional Resources on the Board's Role in Fundraising

Topic	Country	Source Website
The Board's Role in Fundraising	U.S.A.	Nonprofit Research Collaborative http://www.urban.org/UploadedPDF/412673-The-Nonprofit-Research-Collaborative-Special-Report.pdf
		Georgia Center for Nonprofits http://www.gcn.org/articles/what-role-do-boards-and-individual-board-members-have-in-nonprofit-fundraising
		Streamlink Software http://www.streamlinksoftware.com/blog/bid/111577/Nonprofit-Board-Member-Fundraising-Challenges-and-Opportunities
		Zimmerman Lehman, Consultants http://www.zimmerman-lehman.com/specificresponsibilities.htm
		Guidestar http://www2.guidestar.org/rxa/news/articles/2008/five-fundraising-mistakes-we-make-with-our-boards.aspx
		http://www2.guidestar.org/rxa/news/articles/2008/myths-and-realities-of-board-members-and-fundraising.aspx
		http://www2.guidestar.org/rxa/news/articles/2008/fired-up-board-preparing-your-board-members-for-fundraising.aspx
		http://www2.guidestar.org/rxa/news/articles/2008/four-steps-to-take-board-members-from-fear-of-fundraising-to-enthusiasm.aspx
	Australia	BoardConnect http://boardconnect.com.au/resources/publications/399-whos-asking-for-what-fundraising-and-leadership-in-australian-non-profits-qut.html
Fundraising Fundamentals	U.S.A.	Andrew Olsen http://www.andrewolsen.net/best-practices/
		National Council of Nonprofits http://www.councilofnonprofits.org/resources/resources-topic/fundraising
		North Carolina Center for Nonprofits http://www.handsonnwnc.org/express/Fact%20Sheet%20by%20NC%20Center%20on%20Fundraising.pdf
		Ter Molen Watkins and Bandt http://twbfundraising.com/blog/?p=381

Topic	Country	Source Website
	U.S.A and Canada	Fundraising.com http://www.fundraising.com/non-profit-fundraising.aspx
	Canada	Redbird Communications http://www.redbirdonline.com/ blog/16-powerful-online-fundraising-tools-raising-money-and-awareness
	Britain	KnowHow NonProfit http://knowhownonprofit.org/funding/fundraising

Chapter 6

The Board's Structure and Operating Procedures

Symptoms

One of the major, yet often unrecognized, influences on how well a nonprofit organization board carries out its duties and responsibilities is the way it is organized. All boards have at least a minimum amount of formal organization and a set of policies that constrain, and support the way they operate. For example, most nonprofits have a constitution and/or a set of by-laws among which are rules regarding the role of the board, its size and composition, when and how annual meetings will be held, who has voting rights, etc. In addition, most boards create their own operating manuals (or have a collection of documents) that cover such matters as how many and what kind of board committees and board officer positions will exist and so on.

Once these kinds of structures and procedures are in place they often come to be taken for granted and their influence on the way the board governs goes unrecognized. This means they are not carefully examined when boards seek to improve their own performance and orient new members.

A high percentage of agreement with the following statements indicates a board that might have formal structures and operating procedures that are inhibiting its effectiveness:

- [ ] The by-laws that provide the rules within which the board operates are in need of a thorough review.

- [ ] We don't have a board policy manual or we have one that is badly in need of revision.

- [ ] The board seems too large and cumbersome to enable it to act as an effective decision-making body.

- [ ] Job descriptions for the positions of board members and board officers (e.g., Chair, Vice-Chair, Treasurer, Secretary, etc.) are nonexistent or not well understood.

- [ ] Administrative support for the board (secretarial assistance, record keeping, assistance in arranging meetings, etc.) is inadequate.

☐ The board lacks access to potentially useful information and communications technology (e.g. computers, software, internet, the web and social media).

☐ Most board members don't make much use of the information and communications technology made available to them.

☐ Some board committees are not very useful.

☐ Some board committees are unclear about their responsibilities and/or authority.

☐ Some board officers and chairs of committees lack the training or experience needed to meet the demands of their position.

☐ Some committees have members who contribute very little or don't have enough experience to be of much help.

In essence, these items can be clustered in two categories: Procedures and Structures.

1. Issues related to matters of *procedure*:
   - The organization's constitution and by-laws within which the board must operate;
   - Board manuals that contain basic information on the board's responsibilities and operating procedures;
   - Position descriptions for board members and officers of the board; and
   - The nature and extent of administrative and technical support provided to assist the board in carrying out its work efficiently.
2. Issues related to the *formal structure* of the board:
   - Board size;
   - Officer positions;
   - Committees—number, function, authority.

Diagnosis

Why do boards experience problems with inadequate structures and procedures? There are three basic explanations for these problems:

- The most common is simply that boards fail to pay attention to the existing tools that have already been created to help them govern. When boards first come into existence they usually begin in a friendly, informal way. Creating a lot of rules and procedures seems unnecessary as everyone wants to focus on doing whatever they can to help the organization succeed. As the organization grows and the management of the organization professionalizes (i.e. it becomes necessary to create separate positions and introduce paid executives), the board often fails to realize that it, too, needs to become more professional. Instead, the original culture of informality tends to dominate governance practices without anyone realizing it even though it is no longer suitable for dealing with the growing complexity of the organization and its environment. The kinds of boards that are most likely to "drift" without being conscious of the need to update structures and procedures are those which do not make time for assessing their own performance and which do not provide training and development for their members on their roles as governors.

- A lack of focus on developing optimum structures and procedures can also occur when the leadership provided by the board chair and/or the CEO is not conscious of the negative impact that arises when people are unclear about what to do or get into conflicts because by-laws are confusing or absent all together. In a few cases it is possible that those in leadership positions might actively seek to dominate the board by unofficially blocking attempts to increase clarity and transparency in board procedures.
- A similar situation can arise when boards become dominated by an informal "core group" of insiders (for example a dominating Executive Committee or group of "old hands" who hold informal "backstage" meetings to predetermine board votes on contentious issues.

Treatment

Procedural Issues

Constitution and by-laws

Most nonprofit organizations that become incorporated must submit to the government body that approves incorporation a copy of their constitution and by-laws. Various publications or websites exist which provide things like sample by-laws. *Note that specific requirements for the content of by-laws can vary by governmental jurisdictions—national, state or provincial.*

An example of the kinds of questions that each board needs to answer for itself, based on its analysis of its own unique environment and history, is that regarding terms of office for board members and officers of the board. Generally, it is desirable to infuse boards with "new blood" at regular intervals. This can be assured by having a by-law specifying how long a board member's term of office will be and how many times it can be renewed before the incumbent must leave the board. A clause specifying term lengths of two or three years, renewable two or three times is common. In the absence of such a statement, it is often assumed board members can serve indefinitely, which can be problematic.

There are instances, however, when specifying term limits *could* be unwise; for example, when it is clear that there is a relatively small pool of qualified candidates to draw from. The same problem holds true for officer positions, e.g. Chair, Treasurer, etc. Is it good for the board to have the same leadership team year after year? Generally, no, but sometimes it is difficult to replace certain people, such as treasurers. In cases like this, by-laws can be written with qualifying words like "*normally* the term of office for board officers will be three years." This allows a board to make exceptions to the rule if necessary.

Other examples of by-law variations for which there is no "one best rule" and which therefore need to be thought out in the light of the organization's unique history and environment are:

- Definitions of who can and cannot be a member of the organization and vote at general membership meetings;
- How to remove members from the board and organization;
- The authority of members—what they must approve;
- Quorums for board meetings and annual meetings;

- Matters which can be decided by members attending the annual meeting versus those that must be put to a vote of the whole membership via mail ballots, etc.;
- The nature and extent of board decisions that can be made via telephone conference calls, email voting, etc.; and how to amend by-laws

Whatever the board decides with respect to by-laws, it is helpful to have an attorney familiar with nonprofit law in the local jurisdiction advise the board on them. For example, new regulations have emerged in some jurisdictions that require board procedures to be in compliance with the law in such matters as electronic voting, auditing of financial statements, records of minutes, retention of documents and conflict of interest policies. Many legal cases concerning governance decisions have been decided on the basis of the board not following them. See the following link for a nonprofit case concerning by-laws: http://www.501c3.org/blog/why-nonprofit-bylaws-matter-a-tragic-tale/

Board manual

While general guidelines on what to put in by-laws are useful, due to the number and diversity of nonprofits that exist, there are still many decisions that need to be made for which there are no universally agreed to rules of thumb. These kinds of issues should be identified and addressed in a Board Manual. This important document is invaluable for new board members to orient them to the governance role and how the board works but it is also crucial in resolving occasional disputes over how the board should handle various matters.

Position descriptions for board members and officer/committee chair positions

For many small nonprofit organizations, the idea of having written "job descriptions" for board members and officer positions such as the Chair or President, Treasurer, Vice-Chair, and Chairs of various committees may seem unnecessarily bureaucratic and formal. And indeed this might be the case especially if there is little likelihood that people might get into conflict over who has what authority After all, the desired culture most people want in a board is one of collegiality where anybody is willing to lend a hand with anything that needs doing without getting fussy over whose territory it is.

On the other hand, if no effort is made to clarify who is responsible for getting things done, even the most well-meaning team can get into trouble with things "falling between the cracks" or being duplicated. For this reason, for most nonprofits, the time required to develop, and periodically review, position descriptions is worth the effort. Position description documents, which could be incorporated into the Board Manual, should cover:
- The responsibilities of the position—the work it does;
- The authority that goes with the position—what matters the holder of the position is able to decide and what matters need to be decided by the board as a whole or other office holders; and
- The qualifications and competencies required for carrying out the responsibilities of the position.

Administrative support

One of the major conditions that can lead boards to feeling ineffective is inefficient internal administrative support—minutes are not taken or not done well, records of past decisions on who is going to do what and when are not kept, meetings are poorly organized or there is not enough support to prepare for them, etc. If budgets permit, investment in professional staff to support the board is well worth it. If there is no money for paid staff, the next best approach is to clearly define the role of the volunteer board secretary as the *de facto* administrator then seek a volunteer who is well organized and at least somewhat detail oriented and provide them with adequate training and the equipment and supplies needed to do the job well. Time taken to develop simple, well-organized record systems is also well spent.

Another important aspect of the internal administration of the board that is often neglected is the extent to which it makes full use of the potential of modern information and communications technology, i.e. Internet, intranet, online calendars, video-conferencing, voice over Internet-Protocol (e.g. Skype), email, social media, etc.

Boards should consider three questions when making technological decisions:

- For what purposes are modern information and communications technology (ICT) tools needed?
- Do we have the capacity to implement and support the use of them in our board and organization (e.g. can volunteers use them, be trained to use them, or do we need to hire people)?
- Which tools are most likely to return the greatest value for the investment of time and effort?

In work on ICT use by boards, Harrison (2014) concludes that the key to getting the most value out of a technology is to think of it as a means to an end in terms of meeting strategic performance objectives. Once performance objectives have been established (a committee of the board or task force could develop them) and agreed upon (at the whole board level), strategies should be implemented to achieve them. With respect to future strategies, nonprofits should consider enterprise-wide solutions to align strategic and operational work. Boards need to assess the scalability and flexibility of proposed technology in order to facilitate governance and other functions. In the governance context this means the capacity of ICT tools to meet, store documents, share information, communicate, conduct performance assessments, facilitate opinion surveys, engage constituents, etc.

Board Structures

There are three important aspects of the basic formal structure of the board that, if they are improperly designed for the board's situation, can cause major problems: (a) the size of the board; the number and nature of formal "officer positions" within the board; and (c) its committee structure.

(a) Board size

The "how-to" books on boards are fairly consistent in warning against boards that exceed 15 or so people. This recommendation arises because the greater the number of people involved in the complex business of setting strategic direction (the board's number one responsibility), the more difficult it will be to give them meaningful roles and arrive at a consensus on contentious issues. Conversely, the smaller the number involved, the more difficult it will be to get valid representation of the views of the community the organization is serving or, in the case of working boards, enough people to carry out the work of the board. It may also be too easy for "group think" to take hold (a feeling that one should not criticize if the majority share the same point of view) thus keeping out radical ideas for change.

Nevertheless, large boards (e.g. 20 to 30 or even more) do exist. They often occur in part because it is believed that this is the way to gain the support of a lot of influential community leaders who will be useful in raising money and for other purposes. They are also common in national NPOs that feel the need to have representation on the board from many geographical regions. However, it should be realized that it is possible to get the support of prestigious people or input from all regions without resorting to the creation of unwieldy sized boards. One of the more common alternatives is to create advisory boards or funding campaign "cabinets" or "committees."

Even large boards can be effective, however, as long as everyone recognizes and accepts that a smaller subset of board members will probably evolve to play a leadership role. Meetings of the whole board will tend to be dominated by a "core group" and others will usually have to be satisfied with less input on issues though ample opportunity for input should always be provided. The contributions from non-core-group members will come mostly at the individual and committee levels. At these levels they can provide useful advice or contacts on request though, as noted, the same thing could be provided in other ways.

Equally problematic is the very small board (five or fewer) where there is a real risk that the board will not become aware of changing conditions that threaten the organization. They are also not very effective when the board needs to be a working board. Members tend to become overloaded with work and "burn out" can occur rapidly. However, many small boards are not necessarily a problem until a crisis hits. To cope in such situations requires the small board to ensure that it has independent sources of information and expert outside advice on how the organization is doing.

(b) Formal offices

The generally accepted recommendation is to keep formal offices few in number on the grounds that many of them have no real function other than ceremonial. At minimum, however, there must be a board leader (chair, president), and someone (usually a vice-chair) to step in if the leader cannot perform her or his duties as well as learn the ropes to take over when the current leader's term is up. A skilled treasurer is also a very important office with the role of taking the lead in carrying out the fiscal oversight responsibility of the board. As discussed above, the office of board secretary is important because of its record keeping and document retention function. Wherever possible, however, it is usually preferable to have professional staff employed to support board leadership and administrative functions. The main point is that these *functions* must be performed; the actual titles used are not so important. For example, in some small, simple organizations all functions might reside in the offices of chair and vice-chair.

Other formal leadership positions are usually the chairs of the board committees discussed below. The important requirement of all formal offices is that there be clear descriptions of the duties of the office and that provision be made for training those who fill these positions. Too often office holders take up their jobs without a clue as to what is required. With luck, they can learn by on the job trial and error before a major issue arises, otherwise they can get themselves and their organization into serious trouble.

(c) Board committees

At one extreme in the "how-to" literature on boards are those writers who state that the number of committees of the board should be kept to an absolute minimum. It is argued that some committees do more harm than good because they either try to dabble in operations, thereby subverting the authority of managers, or make decisions on policy issues that are the responsibility of the whole board or the CEO. The board and committees therefore end up duplicating each other's work and wasting everyone's time. These are real problems, but eliminating committees is not the only approach to solving them. In fact, in smaller organizations with small budgets unable to hire paid staff to manage all its programs and functions, committees may be vital to the operation of the organization.

There are two basic types of committees:

Policy committees

These are small problem-solving groups, which can study important issues in depth and produce reports for the whole board with recommendations and supporting data. Note that they do *not* decide on policies, they only make recommendations to those with the authority to do so, i.e. the board as a whole.

Working committees

These are policy implementation groups which either assist paid staff in carrying out tasks that staff cannot do alone or are used instead of paid staff because none are available. Some argue that, strictly speaking, such operational committees should not be considered as committees of the board of directors, rather they should report only to managers. This is fine in theory but, in many organizations with working or mixed model boards, the best people to head such committees are already board members. Besides, in doing their work, operational committees often must make decisions that have large-scale implications. These kinds of policy issues must be recognized and brought to the whole board for discussion. Trained and sensitive board members as committee chairs may well be the best judges of whether a major operational issue has strategic implications or not.

Even in governance-only boards, some working committees may be needed at times to help with new operational activities in which the management has little experience, e.g. implementing shared services or a merger with another organization, a new kind of fundraising activity, implementation of a pay equity program, property acquisition or investment decisions.

This said there is much to support the commonly offered recommendation that *standing committees* (i.e. permanent committees created by the organization's by-laws) be kept to a minimum. Too many committees with titles such as Property Committee, Program Committee, Purchasing Committee, etc., may have no clear function as either policy or working committees. Instead they waste the time of managers who have to think of things for them to do when they are not really needed, or they necessarily confuse the lines of authority of both managers and the whole board.

Many consultants urge that standing committees be replaced by *task forces* or *special project groups* to be created on an "as needed" basis with very clear terms of reference and deadlines for doing their jobs, after which they disappear. It is important to note that a big advantage of temporary task forces of the board is that well-qualified non-board members can more easily augment their membership. At the extreme, only the chair need be a board member to bring any policy issues to the board.

Should boards using the governance-only board model have any standing committees, then? Since giving strategic direction is a key board responsibility, a good argument can be made for a *planning committee* to work with other strategically-oriented groups in the organization (such as the management team). It would work with these other groups to help define the issues, assemble relevant information and lay out strategic options for the whole board to consider.

Often the role of taking the lead in strategic planning is played by the *executive committee* so it is worth saying a few words about the risks and benefits of such a committee. An executive committee is usually made up of those holding formal offices on the board (e.g. President, V. P., Treasurer, Secretary etc.) and, in some cases, the chairs of standing committees. Its formal role is usually to look after board business between meetings and set the agenda for board meetings. The pitfall with executive committees is that they can become a powerful "inner cabinet" that arbitrarily makes decisions the board should make and filters the way issues are put before the board so as to favour a predetermined position. For this reason, some board experts advise against the existence of such a committee. On the other hand, someone must perform the function of setting the board agenda and ensuring that everything that goes before the board is of sufficient importance and is well enough prepared and supported with good information. Leaving these matters solely up to the Board Chair and/or CEO increases the possibility of just these two becoming the overly powerful "inner circle." Hence an executive committee with strictly limited powers as to what it can decide is probably a worthwhile entity especially for governance-only boards.

Because the board's responsibility for fiscal oversight is so critical, there is also usually need for a *finance committee,* provided it can be kept from making *de facto* strategic decisions when it reviews the accounts and budgets. Organizations with unique characteristics may well identify other areas where constant operational assistance from volunteer directors is required, thereby necessitating standing committees.

Finally, most boards need help to ensure that they manage themselves well. This self-help is sometimes provided in part by a standing committee of the board such as a *nominating committee*. It attempts to locate the best possible people to stand as potential board members. The trouble is that the conventional nominating committee does not go far enough. Who will arrange to have new board members oriented and trained? Who will take the lead in assessing the board's performance or deal with the cases of individual board members who fail to live up to the role expectations? In some cases, these very important matters are the responsibility of the executive committee. In others, the terms of reference of the nominating committee are expanded and it is renamed as, for example, the "Board Development" or, better, the "Governance Committee."

Table 6 contains links to additional useful information and resources to increase the governance effectiveness of the organization through board structures and procedures.

Table 6

Additional Resources Related to Board Structures and Procedures

Topic	Country	Source Website
General Board Structures	U.S.A.	The Bridgespan Group http://www.bridgespan.org/Publications-and-Tools/Nonprofit-Boards/Nonprofit-Boards-101/Nonprofit-Board-Structure.aspx#.U2bn0oFdX84

Topic	Country	Source Website
		U.S. Internal Revenue Service http://form1023.org/how-to-draft-nonprofit-bylaws-with-examples
		The Foundation Group http://501c3.org/blog/nonprofit-bylaws-the-dos-and-donts/
		Mondaq http://www.mondaq.com/unitedstates/x/287604/Charities+Non-Profits/New+York+NonProfit+Revitalization+Act
	Canada	Public Legal Education Association of Saskatchewan http://www.plea.org/legal_resources/?a=259&searchTxt=incorporation&cat=28&pcat=4
	Britain	KnowHow NonProfit http://knowhownonprofit.org/leadership/governance/governance-structure-and-roles/trustee-board-composition-and-structure
Board Policy Manuals	U.S.A.	Free Management Library http://managementhelp.org/boards/manual.htm
	Canada	Industry Canada https://www.ic.gc.ca/eic/site/cilp-pdci.nsf/vwapj/Primer_en.pdf/$FILE/Primer_en.pdf
	Canada	Muttart Foundation http://www.muttart.org/sites/default/files/downloads/publications/drafting_revising.pdf
Position Descriptions for Board Members and Officers	U.S.A	Free Management Library http://managementhelp.org/boards/manual.htm
Board Committees	U.S.A.	Free Management Library http://managementhelp.org/boards/manual.htm
		Blue Avocado http://www.blueavocado.org/content/boards-should-only-have-three-committees

Topic	Country	Source Website
Board Administrative Support	Canada	Ontario Ministry of Agriculture and Food http://www.omafra.gov.on.ca/english/rural/facts/08-059.htm
Conflict of Interest Policies for Boards	U.S.A.	Nonprofit Risk Management Center http://www.nonprofitrisk.org/library/articles/board120307.shtml
		National Council of Nonprofits http://www.councilofnonprofits.org/conflict-of-interest
	Canada	Community Sector Council of Newfoundland and Labrador http://communitysector.nl.ca/board-development/conflict-interest-policy
	Australia	Australian Centre for Philanthropy and Nonprofit Studies https://wiki.qut.edu.au/display/CPNS/Conflict+of+interest+policy

Chapter 7

Effective Board Meetings

Symptoms

For most people with little experience with boards of directors, the belief is that the main work of boards takes place at its official, formal meetings. In actual fact a great deal of important board work takes place before and after those meetings. Nevertheless, the quality of formal board meetings can make a considerable difference to a board's success. At the very least, having to sit in on a number of poorly run meetings can destroy the commitment of even the most dedicated supporter of an organization's cause. Meetings that are poorly organized, go on too long, go off on tangents instead of sticking to the point, feature personal conflicts or domineering individuals turn people off and can cause serious damage by leading to poorly considered decisions.

A high percentage of agreement with the following statements indicates a board that might have problems in carrying out its meetings effectively and efficiently.

☐ The agenda for board meetings does not get into the hands of board members in time for them to familiarize themselves with the issues before the meeting.

☐ When the agenda does come, there is too much information to digest or not enough to adequately familiarize board members about the issues.

☐ The agenda for meetings is too full of "routine" motions or items "for information only" so there isn't time to discuss more important matters.

☐ The agenda items of greatest importance often come up too late in the meeting when board members are too tired to concentrate on them.

☐ We have problems when it comes to attendance at board meetings; too many members miss too many meetings.

☐ Board meetings often go on too long.

☐ Once the board has finished discussing something, it is not clear who is going to do what and when.

☐ There is too much unconstructive arguing among some members during meetings.

☐ Meetings are run too informally, for example with more than one person talking at once, no time limits on discussions, etc.

☐ Meetings stick too much to formal "rules of order" so that thorough, probing discussions are discouraged.

☐ A few members seem to dominate discussions and this discourages quieter board members from contributing.

In essence, problems with board meetings can be grouped under five headings:

1. Agenda clarity and timing

Critical to the success of any formal meeting is having a clear agenda that organizes the planned content of the meeting. Also, if the agenda document is delivered to participants too late (or, even worse, is not made available until the beginning of the meeting), people cannot prepare adequately.

2. Supporting information

There is also a need for the agenda to contain enough documentation on the matters to be discussed to get everyone "up to speed" on them before they are brought up. Nothing renders a board ineffective more than members scrambling to read important materials at the same time as an issue is being discussed or, worse, not having important material available for them to read beforehand.

On the other hand, it is also possible to provide *too much* in the way of supporting materials with agendas—materials that are not really relevant to the matter at hand but that the agenda preparers misguidedly think "might be useful." The regrettable tendency of many board members, when faced with a huge pile of documents that do not obviously relate to the issues at hand, is to give it a glance at best.

3. Meeting content

The most common problems with board meetings is that too much time is spent listening to reports "for information only" (i.e., that do not require any decisions other than a motion to "accept the report"), or discussing matters that could better be discussed and decided upon by the CEO and her/his management team or a committee of the board. The ideal meeting puts the most important matters requiring motions and decisions as close to the top of the agenda as possible and provides enough time for careful deliberation.

To be sure, *some* of the matters that are "for information only" could be conceived of as necessary in that they help the board carry out its due diligence function of ensuring that everything is running well and according to plan. Identifying these matters requires careful thought. However, certain reports from committees or managers may not necessarily have to actually take up the time of board meetings to deal with them unless they contain motions requiring board level decisions (see discussion of "consent agendas" under "Treatment" below).

4. Clarity and effectiveness of decisions made at board meetings

Even when the agenda and the meeting content are well-designed, board meetings can be less than successful if the decision-making process is flawed. For example:

- Meetings that are dominated by a small group of "talkers" while quieter members with useful things to say are not drawn into the conversation;
- Not enough time is scheduled for a full discussion of an issue;
- The discussion goes off on tangents that are not relevant to the issue;
- Decisions are reached but lack clarity about who is going to do what and when;
- No follow up is provided to permit the board to check on progress made in implementing decisions taken at prior meetings.

5. Attendance

If there are problems with meetings in any or all of the four areas discussed above, they may result in poor attendance at board meetings—too many people missing too many meetings. Whatever the cause of poor meeting attendance, it is a good indicator of possible problems in the way the board is working.

Diagnosis

Since very few people like taking part in meetings that are too long, confusing or boring, why do so many boards seem to get into situations where this is exactly what happens? The simplest explanation is that these practices become part of the culture of the board and no one seems to recognize that they could be changed. Typically, when a nonprofit organization is young and being run by a small handful of enthusiasts who are willing to do anything and everything needed to keep things going, informal board meetings that deal with everything and have to move quickly from crisis to crisis are common. As the organization evolves and professionalizes to the extent that it can afford to hire a paid CEO or develop committees to whom things can be delegated with confidence, the old meeting practices of the board fail to change even though they become more and more inappropriate for the situation.

Another major reason for poor meetings is lack of a good meeting facilitator in the role of the board chair. Our research and that of a few others on the role and impact of the board chair suggests that meetings become ineffective when the chair is either under-controlling (lets the meeting get off track, or allows a few members to dominate) or over-controlling (the meeting becomes very formal and rigid). Poor chairing can occur when the skills and aptitude needed for effective meeting leadership are overlooked when choosing a chair or the chair has not had time to develop the skills needed for the role. Meeting management skills are very learnable if proper training is provided but many of those who end up accepting nomination for the Chair or President role may not see they need to develop them. A more detailed discussion of the role of the Chair appears in the chapter on Leadership in these Guidelines.

Sometimes the reason for ineffective board meetings, unfortunately, is the presence of a CEO (paid top manager) who, consciously or unconsciously, does not want a strong board but rather one that is dependent on him/her for information and guidance in all its deliberations. Such CEOs can provide too little information on important issues which leads to "rubber-stamp" decision-making. Conversely some CEOs try to manipulate their boards by providing too much information—"a snow job." They can also bias the information that is provided so as to favor one position on an issue over another. Also, they can strongly influence the selection of new board members so as to ensure that only those with the same point of view on issues as themselves are chosen. All of these actions by CEOs can reduce board effectiveness.

Treatment

The goal of official meetings of the whole board should be to focus on issues that have implications for the strategic direction of the organization or that create understanding about an issue or situation the organization is facing. Even with a clear focus on matters of strategic importance, the effectiveness of boards can be influenced by a number of factors, including meeting frequency and times, meeting length and design, and meeting rules and attendance.

Meeting Frequency and Times

There is definitely no fixed rule about the optimum frequency of official meetings of the whole board. Actual practice can vary from monthly to annually. The governing criterion, which can be stated in by-laws or board policy manuals, ought to be that the board should hold a formal meeting when it has enough business to warrant doing so. For example, in working boards, meetings could occur quite often. In governance-only boards, they may occur less often. Chairs and CEOs can recognize if they are calling too many board meetings if they have an attendance problem or if they find themselves thinking, "Another board meeting coming up. How can we fill up the agenda this time?"

In the case of some governance-only boards in very stable environments, meetings might be only three times a year: a meeting to approve the strategic plan; an interim progress report meeting; and an evaluation meeting to assess how well the organization has performed. These, however, are *official decision-making* meetings. But in today's complex governance environment with multiple stakeholders and a fast changing and threat-laden world, it is much more likely that issues will come up that will require boards to come together more often and to interact with people other than themselves and the top management team. In *Governance as Leadership* (2005), Chait, Ryan and Taylor suggest "landmarks" or "characteristics of an issue" boards should recognize as opportunities to engage in what they call "Generative Governing":

- The issue or situation is *ambiguous* or there are multiple perspectives on it;
- The issue or situation is *salient* in that it is important to different people or constituents;
- The issue or situation is *high stakes* in that it relates to the organization's purpose or core values;
- The issue or situation may be *polarizing* and there is a need to bring people together; and
- The issue or situation is *irreversible* in that it cannot be easily changed after a decision is made (p. 107).

For this reason, many nonprofit organizations today find that it is useful to differentiate between decision-making meetings and "information briefing meetings" held for the purpose of becoming informed about a single important strategic issue. These latter meetings are usually characterized by less formal discussions and feature input from invited staff, experts from outside or representatives from clients, members or external stakeholders. Specific motions are not debated; instead, information is provided, alternatives identified and opinions sought. This is all fed to relevant board or management working groups, who then develop specific policy recommendations in the context of the organization's strategic plan. Formal discussion and voting on such recommendations occurs at one of the decision-making board meetings.

The question of the *time of board meetings* is important when board membership is diverse and everyone's time of availability does not fit the same period of the day, or day of the week (mothers caring for children unable to attend midmorning meetings, shift workers unable to attend evening meetings, or others unable to meet on weekdays). The organization must be conscious of the need to vary meeting times in such circumstances so all board members have an equally fair opportunity to attend. It is also worth considering the use of modern communications technology such as conference calls, Skype, and online meeting applications etc., as a means of allowing participation by those not able to physically attend.

Meeting Length

Another indicator of board meeting mismanagement is meeting length. The span of time that the average person can focus on complex decision-making tasks without losing their clarity of thought is no longer than 50 minutes, though this can be extended somewhat with refreshment breaks. Board meetings that regularly last longer than two hours can be an indication of problems. Either too much time is being spent on issues that do not need to be considered by the whole board or there are too many items that involve long-winded reports "for information only." Alternatively, the regular occurrence of long debates that extend meeting times may indicate badly-worded motions or poorly-prepared reports that do not contain enough supporting data. When these kinds of long discussions occur often, attention should be paid to how to improve the work of the committees or managers who prepare the agenda items in question.

Occasionally, some CEOs seeking rubber stamp approval of their recommendations on contentious issues deliberately create long agendas. They then insure that the issues they want the board to rubber stamp are placed at the *end*. By that time, no one has the energy to think, let alone discuss and object.

The "consent agenda" option

When board meetings go on too long because too many of the items being presented are "for information only," a solution increasingly adopted by many is the introduction of a "consent agenda." The following is an example of the use of a consent agenda suggested by board expert David Renz (2006):

> When a by-law or some other rule or regulation requires formal approval by the board, yet there is no value added by engaging the board in discussion about the item (e.g., a routine lease renewal for a facility already included in the approved agency budget). The procedure is to have all items of this type sent beforehand to board members. When these items come up at the meeting, there is no oral presentation or discussion of the information. Instead, it is taken as understood that the information has been reviewed by members beforehand and will only be discussed if anyone has a question or wants to comment on it.

> Consent agenda items are usually put forward at the beginning of the meeting. Use of a consent agenda can save large amounts of time though the disadvantage is that it might hurt the feelings of those who prepared the reports and would like to have their "moment in the sun" before the whole board. A conscious effort to recognize and praise the work of

individuals and committees that prepare material that is included in a consent agenda can help mitigate this problem.

Another tactic for controlling the length of meetings is to have the agenda preparers estimate the length of time that will be needed for presentation and discussion of each item and insert the "estimated time" on the agenda document. These estimates should be treated as guidelines only, however. Sometimes issues end up requiring more than the time allocated to them. Rather than arbitrarily cutting off important discussion, it is better for the Chair to ask permission of the meeting to extend the time, then either postpone discussion of less important matters or reduce the discussion time on them.

The flip side of meetings that go on too long is the meeting that ends too soon. Meetings that the board rushes through in, say, half an hour could be an indication of a rubber stamp board. If this happens regularly it might be that the board has been conditioned not to question whatever is put before it or simply that there should be fewer meetings.

Meeting Design

As discussed above, one of the most common complaints of board members is that meetings are "not properly organized." Specific problems include the following:

- The agenda does not reach board members until very shortly before, or even at, the meeting so they have no time to prepare;
- The agenda contains too much information that is irrelevant to the issues to be discussed *or* there is not enough relevant information;
- The order of the agenda items places unimportant and routine items at the top while important ones are at the end, when energy tends to run out;
- Meetings fail to follow accepted "rules of order" so can become too disorganized; *or*, conversely, are too formal or rule bound, thereby discouraging full and frank debate.

Except in rare emergency situations, there is really no excuse for not getting agendas into the hands of board members three to five working days before the meeting. It is often helpful when planning the content of the Agenda to request board members to submit suggestions for matters needing discussion. Agendas should be organized so that items requiring decisions are put at the top. All supporting material should be directly relevant to the impending discussion.

Meeting Rules

Even the most informal working boards should adopt one of the standard authorities on "rules of order" for meetings, such as Roberts Rules (http://www.robertsrules.org/rulesintro.htm) to be used as a guide in conducting official board meetings. It is also important that the Chair, or a designated other person, be familiar with these rules and how they are applied. This, however, does not mean that all meetings must be run in strict accordance with these "parliamentary" rules. The rules are primarily of benefit when the items to be discussed are likely to be highly controversial with a lot of disagreement among board members. As in any emotion-laden debate, rules are needed to make it fair. These would include: how often a person can speak, rules regarding how amendments to motions can be made, when and how a motion can be tabled, what constitutes being "out of order," etc. In most non-crisis situations, however, a much more relaxed approach can be taken to meeting rules provided the informal culture of the board is one that values an orderly, business-like approach.

Meeting Attendance

Spotty attendance by a high proportion of board members is usually an indication that a significant number of members are dissatisfied with the board and/or their role on it though sometimes it indicates logistical problems like meeting times that don't suit a number of people. Some consultants urge compulsory attendance rules as a way of getting the members out to meetings, e.g., "Members must attend at least 2/3rds of the meetings each year or resign unless a valid excuse is provided and accepted by the Executive Committee." This may get out the members but can mask the real problems behind low commitment.

The Table 7 contains additional useful information and resources to increase the governance effectiveness of the organization through high quality board meetings.

Table 7

Additional Resources to Improve the Quality of Board Meetings

Topic	Country	Source Website
General Guidelines: How to Conduct Effective Meetings	U.S.A.	Free Management Library http://managementhelp.org/misc/meeting-management.htm
		About.com http://nonprofit.about.com/od/boardquestions/a/boardboredom.htm?nl=1
	Australia	Victorian Public Sector Commission http://www.ssa.vic.gov.au/governance/entitys-annual-governance-cycle/internal-reporting-meetings-a-decision-making.html
	Britain	Accounting Web https://www.icsa.org.uk/assets/files/pdfs/090928.pdf
Meeting Planning and Scheduling	U.S.A.	Cause and Effect http://www.ceffect.com/wp-content/uploads/2014/03/board_meeting.pdf
Meeting Rules	U.S.A.	Houston Chronicle http://smallbusiness.chron.com/nonprofit-organization-business-meeting-rules-21608.html
Consent Agendas	U.S.A.	Midwest Center for Nonprofit Leadership http://bloch.umkc.edu/mwcnl/resources/documents/consent-agenda.pdf

Chapter 8

The Composition and Development of the Board

Symptoms

A major component of effective boards is having the right combination of people on them and providing them with ample opportunity to learn what they need to know to be good governors. The two basic requirements for all board members is that they be *committed to the mission* of the organization and have the *time and energy* to devote to the work of the board. After that, the specific mix of leadership competencies that is best for a given board in the environment in which it works can vary greatly from one organization to another. Even though most boards probably have members who get along quite well some may have a sense that, *as a group*, the mix of people might not be ideal. They may feel that the board as a whole is lacking in expertise, is not diverse enough and/or has not received the level of orientation and training it needs to become highly effective. A high percentage of agreement with the following statements indicates that board composition and development might be improved:

☐ Looking at the board as a whole, there is not enough "new blood" coming on to it to bring fresh energy and ideas.

☐ Finding high quality new board members is a problem for us.

☐ We do not pay enough attention to making sure we get the mix of skills and backgrounds we need in the new board members we recruit.

☐ The diversity of public with an interest in this organization is not well represented in the make-up of the board.

☐ We don't do a very good job of orienting and training new board members.

☐ There is not enough ongoing professional development and training for regular board members.

Diagnosis

There are several possible reasons for issues relating to composition and development of the board:

1. As with so many problem areas in board governance, the root of difficulties with the composition of the board may lie in the culture that the board has evolved. Unspoken shared attitudes may exist such as, "We can always find good members just by asking our friends"; or, "It's too hard to find new people so let's just keep the ones we have"; or, "New members can easily learn the ropes just by sitting in on our meetings and watching how we do things." Where do such attitudes come from? Sometimes there are informal subgroups within boards—older members who have been around a long time, for example—whose opinions dominate the rest of the board. Since their selection and training was informal and based on connections to prior board members, they feel there is no need to change.

2. Another source of the difficulty in developing a better mix of members and a trained board is failure to allocate responsibility for doing this to a specific role (e.g., chair) or board committee (e.g., governance committee). Thus, even though the board may sometimes talk about developing the board or recruiting different kinds of new members, it may not be knowledgeable or organized enough to implement those practices.

3. Board by-laws that make no provision for limited terms of office for board members invite the possibility that the board will not attempt to rejuvenate itself.

4. It could also be the case that the board does not carry out regular assessments of its own performance and is thus "blind" to the need for change in board composition selection criteria or development practices.

5. A special kind of blockage to changes in board composition can arise in relatively new organizations dominated by one or more "founding fathers." The problem created is called Founder's Syndrome. It occurs when the founding fathers (or mothers) of the organization have created a culture, like that described above, in which board turnover is believed not to be necessary. Instead, the founders see themselves as the "keepers of the flame" and don't want to risk newcomers making changes in how things are done.

Treatment

To increase the effectiveness of the governance function, consider the following approaches to board composition and development.

Board Composition

Critical to having a successful board is getting the right people on it in the first place. The difficult part is deciding who will be "right" for the organization. Too often the tendency is to appoint members who resemble existing members or who are suitable for conditions as they were but who may not be suitable for a changing future. There is a good deal of advice available to those who are seeking to put together a successful board but there are only two universal criteria which are supported both by research and the "how-to" authors:

1. Board members must be *committed* to the organization's mission, i.e., they must believe strongly in what the organization is trying to do and seriously want to help. A board dominated by people who sit on it as a favor to a friend or because they believe it will look good on their resumé will not usually be effective.

2. Prospective members must have the *time and energy* to devote to the board's business.

Establishing board recruitment needs

The first step in finding the best potential members for a board is to be clear about the kind of people one is seeking in the first place. One way to do this is by compiling a board needs document. Table 8 provides one example of a simple recruitment needs grid that can be used to identify possible composition gaps on the board.

Table 8

Sample Board Member Recruitment Grid

Composition of the Board	Board Members						
Potential Board Effectiveness Criteria	**A**	**B**	**C**	**D**	**E**	**F**	**G**
Stakeholder Connections							
Clients/Users/Audience							
Funders							
Actual/Potential Partners							
Governments or Other Regulators							
Community Leaders							
Business Leaders							
Other							
Useful Skills and Experience							
Fundraising							
Public Relations/Community Relations							
Leadership							
Finance/Accounting							
Planning/Strategy/Innovation							
Legal							
Marketing/Social Media							
Human Resources							
Performance/Project Management							
Data Analytics/IT							
Other							

Demographic Representation Balanced diversity among the desired demographic characteristics such as:							
Gender							
Geographic Location (region, district, state, country)							
Age							
Ethno-Racial Background							
Socio-Economic Background							

Down the left hand column of Table 8 are listed some of the kinds of background characteristics of individuals that might be important to have on the board. The actual characteristics chosen should be decided on by each organization as they might vary depending on local conditions. Across the top of Table 8 are listed the names of the *current* board members. The committee doing the nominating then informally assesses the composition of the board by checking and describing the extent to which each member possesses each of the characteristics in column 1. The board could then be "rated" according to the extent to which it meets these criteria: in terms of being "high" (present board members fulfill each criterion), "medium" (some criteria are met but not all) or "low" (a number of the criteria are not met by the present board members. A careful examination and discussion of the results of this process should give the committee an indication of the "gaps" in desirable background characteristics needed by the board at that time. This becomes the basis for the subsequent recruitment drive.

Note: The needs matrix discussed above will identify potentially useful characteristics in future board members. However, to know that someone possesses a certain qualification or experience does not necessarily mean that they will perform well as a board member. They must be able and willing to 'do', not just 'be'.

There are also many other important questions to answer when it comes to finding the ideal mix of people for a board. The main ones are discussed below.

Should boards be composed primarily of "important" people?

Having many "big name" people on the board can help in giving the organization credibility and a high profile in the community. And some, if not all, "names" have valuable talents. The dilemma is that many of these people may be on other boards or are so busy in their day jobs that they don't really have time to do much more than make token appearances.

Many organizations elect to keep the percentage of "prestige" members relatively small and tolerate minimal involvement as the price that must be paid for their ability to provide contacts and credibility. The majority of the board carries the workload. Of course if the "busy names" become the majority of the board, this can often lead to a rubber stamp board that simply approves recommendations brought to it by management.

The other approach is to put the prestigious names on an "Advisory" or "Honorary" Board comprising those who can give useful help with specific matters (such as fundraising) and heighten the organization's profile but who are not expected to govern.

What is the right amount and kind of diversity to have among board members?

It is generally agreed that boards should represent the diversity of the people that they serve but research has established that many boards do not achieve this representation (Bradshaw, Fredette & Sukornyk, 2009). Instead, the majority of their members have similar demographic and other background characteristics (usually middle class, middle-aged, well-educated, with business or professional experience and of European ethnic origin). To what extent this affects the board, or organization's performance depends on how diverse the populations are that the organization serves. The hypothesis is that a non-representative board will increase the chances that the agency will serve the needs of non-mainstream communities poorly. Put in positive terms, the advantage of expanding a board's diversity along ethno-racial, social class, gender and other dimensions is that this will improve the board's "boundary spanning" function and lead to better strategic leadership.

On the other hand, the fear associated with a very diverse board is that these new kinds of members won't always understand how the board operates and won't be able to make decisions in the best interest of the organization as a whole. Again, there is no research evidence that this frequently happens. Differences in background may sometimes make it more difficult to develop a comfortable, open, problem-solving climate but it is not impossible. Given careful selection of the individual nominees, placement in the "right" role (also known as functional inclusion), and an adequate board development program, a diverse board can be much more effective than a homogeneous one (Fredette & Bradshaw, 2011).

How much should the board be made up of "stakeholders" who have specific interests in the organization, as opposed to more general "community representatives"?

Stakeholders consist of organized interest groups, e.g., on a university board of governors, there would be representation from the student government, the faculty association, government departments, the alumni association, support staff association and associations representing the community. Again, the positive side of organized stakeholder representation is it promotes "bringing the outside in" and "taking the inside out." Once more, the downside risk is the possibility that the representatives will feel they must act solely in what they see as the interests of the organized group they represent. Hard data on the extent to which this actually happens is very scarce. The probability is that problems arise only infrequently, but stakeholder organizations can cause major upheavals during crisis periods such as downsizing, opening or closing programs, or shifting attention from one client group to another. Again, great care in selecting the individual representatives and thorough board training in putting the interests of the organization first can help minimize the frequency of destructive approaches to conflict during periods of change.

How well should candidates know the organization and the field that it is in?

Another dilemma is the extent to which the board should consist of members who already have an in-depth knowledge of what the organization does and how it operates. For boards using the working board model, this is quite important, at least for selection of the majority of their members. For Governing Boards, it may be impossible, other than by choosing internal stakeholder representatives. A majority of Governing Board members will not be "experts" in the organization they govern or the "industry" in which it operates. This raises the question: how can they provide strategic leadership? As noted, the solution to this problem lies in thorough orientation and provision of at least partially independent information systems for the board.

How much should "business skills" be emphasized?

What is the extent to which board members should possess specific skills or knowledge based on their employment or training in areas such as business administration, corporate law, accounting, marketing, human resources, performance management, IT, and public and government relations. One school of thought says this kind of talent is very useful for providing the executive director with invaluable free advice on all sorts of management issues. The other says it is overrated and runs the serious risk of creating a board which is going to be primarily interested in management and unable to focus on governance issues. Again, there are no data to support either of these assertions so probably there is not a universally correct mix. Organizations with working and mixed model boards are, by definition, deficient in certain operational leadership and management skills so board members who can help fill such gaps are important. Even in large professionally managed institutions there can be certain areas of specialized knowledge that the organization cannot afford to pay for but which a board member might possess. As a general rule, it is wise to be aware of the skill, knowledge and abilities of the Executive Director and his/her management team. The better they are, the less need for board members to fill gaps. When it *is* necessary to select board members with specific skills, the key is to train these useful specialists to understand that their expertise will be sought in the roles of advisors or implementers only, not as decision-makers.

A note on the need for board candidates being willing and able to donate money to the organization

In some cultures and certain nonprofit organizations that depend heavily on donations from the public or corporations, there is an expectation that board members show their support for the organization by making a personal donation of money. The belief is that showing the public that all board members make donations will help in fundraising appeals. There are two points to consider when thinking about making board member donations a criterion for member selection:
- Though most professional fundraisers tend to believe that publicizing a unanimous board donation record makes a difference to how much external donors will give, there is no actual evidence from empirical research showing that this is so.
- If showing unanimous donor support *is* deemed to be necessary, it is not necessary for such donations to be large. They need only be what each member is willing and able to afford.

What individual personal qualities to look for?

Developing broad criteria for board selection such as those discussed above is important but, in the end, the most important criteria are those that are the most difficult to specify and measure in potential candidates for membership. These are the *personality characteristics* that one wants to see in board members. Everyone who has ever spent much time watching different boards come and go in an organization will agree that, some years, the majority of board members seem particularly quick to understand issues, be creative and constructive in their handling of differences and business-like, while in other years the opposite qualities prevail. Since most boards don't like to check carefully into the personal qualities of the people they nominate, it is almost a matter of chance how well the mix works out in any particular year.

What is needed, clearly, is: (a) an attempt to articulate the kinds of personality characteristics and personal values that are being sought and (b) a serious attempt to state how they will be discerned in any given nominee. Under heading (a), the following are some of the qualities that we found were associated with high impact leadership on nonprofit boards:

- Honest, helpful, and humble.
- Self and socially aware.
- Able to "see the big picture."
- Creative and open to change.
- Able to communicate, work well with others, and handle conflict respectfully.

Regarding (b), there is not enough space here to provide a full review of the most valid methods for assessing these characteristics in people; most textbooks on human resource management will do that. Suffice it to say here that the essence of the process lies in how the candidates' past behavior is checked through references. This process needs to be systematically thought out in advance and implemented with care. The all-too-common method of nominating someone whom one other board member believes "is a wonderful person" just is not good enough. These days, most people called to provide references are loath to communicate negative things especially in writing. However, some might be more open sharing useful information in response to oral conversations in which they are asked questions that relate to specific actions, e.g., "What role did 'x' play in your strategic planning process?" or "How was 'x' involved in your fundraising activities?"

A carefully designed board recruitment process looks something like this:

- It is carried out by a Governance (or Nominations) committee of the board.
- The committee looks at the strengths of the existing board and tries to identify gaps in skills, abilities and background that need to be filled.
- A widely broadcast call for nominations is made highlighting the qualifications sought.
- Those making nominations are asked informally to provide information on why their candidate(s) is suitable using the criteria in Table 8.
- Those who are willing to act as references for the potential nominee should be asked how they perceive him/her in specific situations.
- A short list of suitable nominees is created and ranked as strong, medium or weak candidates. Each person on the list would then be approached by the board chair in the order in which they are ranked.

The special problems of low profile organizations

Unfortunately, for a large number of worthy but low-profile organizations that support less popular causes, the problem of board composition is not one of how to choose among a range of possible candidates; rather it is to find enough people of any kind who meet the basic criteria of commitment to the organization's mission and willingness to devote enough time and effort to the cause. This is a problem of recruitment, rather than selection. Solving it requires developing a focused, formal recruitment program for board members.

The usual method employed by successful nonprofits of this type is the "grow-your-own" approach. This is accomplished by concentrating on getting a lot of working volunteers to help with programs and projects. The best of these are then identified and systematically wooed and trained to accept increasing amounts of responsibility, including the leadership of others. Before long, those with skills and attitudes required on the board can be asked to join it (which, in these situations, is almost always a working board). In desperation, one can trust recruitment to the efforts of a few board members to pressure their friends to join, but don't expect a very effective board as a result.

A final word on board composition

Though there are no hard and fast rules about how a board should be made up, there is probably one generalization that fits all voluntary organizations that are facing rapidly changing, often threatening, environments: strive for balanced diversity. The exact *kind* of mix will vary from situation to situation, but a mix it should be. Older, younger; men, women; rich, poor; "old hands," "young blood"; business and non-business backgrounds; multi-ethnic and multi-racial—the criteria can vary. But only with a balanced mix can the organization improve its chances for getting the fresh ideas and specialized information it needs to cope with its changing world. Remember, however, that to make it all work, the board needs training in how to work together as a team and in how to discern the greater good of the organization as the basis for making all decisions.

Board Development

Even though boards may manage to find the ideal mix of skilled and committed people to become members, they may still end up losing some of them or having them perform ineffectively. This may be because members do not know what is expected of them, or lack the skill and knowledge needed to make good decisions in the governor role. The most direct way to deal with this problem is through a well-planned system of board orientation, development and evaluation (Brown, 2007, Brudney & Murray, 1998; Green & Gresinger, 1996; Herman, 2005; Herman & Renz, 1998, 1999; Herman, Renz & Heimovics, 1997; Holland & Jackson, 1998; Brudney & Nobbie, 2002). The components of such a system are:

- A board manual which provides full background information on the organization and its articles of incorporation and by-laws, current programs and plans, descriptions of the position of board members, and outlines of the responsibilities of board officers and committees, and minutes of recent board meetings.
- A formal orientation program at which new board members meet top management officials, tour facilities and hear presentations on the organization's programs and background information on strategic issues. Also helpful here are informal "mentoring" programs, which pair new members with current members. A good mentoring program will "train the trainer" by providing the mentor with a checklist of topics to discuss and the necessary information to cover.
- Periodic formal occasions at which the board assesses its own performance, for example by using Board Check-Up or questionnaires covering much the same topics as the content of this guide. Feedback from the management team and staff and stakeholders who interact with the board should also be obtained. Also useful in helping boards get a realistic picture of how they are doing is obtaining periodic

feedback from key external stakeholders on how *they* view the board's work. Differences in perceptions of board effectiveness between the board, staff and external stakeholders are often an indicator of a potentially harmful situation that should be addressed.

Finally, there is value in creating a "buddy system" for new board members in which individual existing board members with good knowledge of how the board and organization works are formally asked to mentor new members during their first year on the board.

There is also a need to assess the performance of individual board members with an eye toward continuous growth and effective support of the organization. This can be done by having board members self-assess their performance informally or through formal analysis of data collected from a questionnaire. It is remarkable how honest many are willing to be. However, attendance records and feedback from the Chair and Committee Heads can also be useful. The main problem is that assessing individual performance often feels like a very awkward thing to do because members are volunteers, have egos and a certain amount of prestige in the community. It is not impossible, however, if board members are shown when they join that there is a formal system of board self-evaluation and understand how the information obtained through it is to be used. This problem can be overcome if the culture of the board is understood to be one of support for each board member in order to help them contribute as best they can. Rather than identifying and concentrating on shortfalls, individual performance discussions can be opportunities to set goals for the coming year, identify areas of interest that the board member may want to expand on and new roles they may assume in order to help the organization prosper.

Table 9 contains additional useful information and resources to increase the governance effectiveness of the organization through board composition and development.

Table 9

Additional Board Composition and Development Resources

Topic	Country	Source Website
Board Composition and Diversity	U.S.A.	Board Source https://www.boardsource.org/eweb/dynamicpage.aspx?webcode=Envision-Your-Ideal-Board
		https://www.boardsource.org/eweb/DynamicPage.aspx?Site=bds2012&WebKey=5f1fc00a-9d38-4362-854b-61a0efe92325
		Creating the Future http://www.help4nonprofits.com/NP_Bd_Diversity_Art.htm
		Blue Avocado http://www.blueavocado.org/node/762

Topic	Country	Source Website
	Britain	KnowHow NonProfit http://knowhownonprofit.org/leadership/governance/governance-structure-and-roles/equality-and-diversity/?searchterm=board%20recruitment http://knowhownonprofit.org/leadership/governance/improving-your-governance-practice/do-we-have-the-right-people-on-board
	Australia	SVA Quarterly http://knowhownonprofit.org/leadership/governance/improving-your-governance-practice/do-we-have-the-right-people-on-board
Board Recruitment	U.S.A.	Free Management Library http://www.managementhelp.org/boards/recruit.htm Board Source https://www.boardsource.org/eweb/DynamicPage.aspx?Site=bds2012&WebKey=0a0a94b4-ccc1-4bc5-893f-8b9d5647c03f https://www.boardsource.org/eweb/DynamicPage.aspx?webcode=Recruit-Board-Members Bridgespan Goup http://www.bridgespan.org/Publications-and-Tools/Hiring-Nonprofit-Leaders/Recruiting-Board-Members/Recruiting-and-Vetting-Nonprofit-Board-Members.aspx#.U2lHvfldW58 Guidestar http://www.guidestar.org/rxa/news/articles/2012/board-recruitment-resources.aspx Center on Public Skill Training http://www.createthefuture.com/developing.htm

Chapter 9

The Informal Culture of the Board

Symptoms

Board culture is the collection of taken-for-granted attitudes, social norms, perceptions and beliefs about "how we do things around here" shared, usually unconsciously, by a majority of board members. A high percentage of agreement with the following statements might indicate problems with the informal culture of the board:

☐ Too many board members seem unwilling to devote much time or effort to the work of the board.

☐ There are many differences of opinion among board members that never get resolved. The board doesn't handle conflict very well.

☐ The board does not regularly and systematically assess its own performance and change itself if it thinks it can improve.

☐ Board members tend not to be involved in representing the organization to the outside community or bringing the concerns of that community into the organization.

☐ As far as I know, many board members have contacts among people who might help the organization but they are not encouraged, or given the opportunity, to make use of them.

☐ Individual board members with skills and knowledge that might be of use to the organization are rarely approached informally for their assistance.

☐ Little effort is made to help board members get to know one another and develop "team spirit" as a group.

Diagnosis

Why do cultures evolve the way they do? There are at least six major sources of influence that can shape board culture without the members being aware of it:

1. Sometimes there are external pressures for boards to act in certain ways that come from critical stakeholder groups such as funders, members or associations of other nonprofit organizations in the same "business."

2. In the case of boards of relatively young organizations or those with a high percentage of new members, certain beliefs, attitudes or social norms may come from founders or members who have previous experience on other boards.

3. Similarly when most board members share a homogenous background in terms of such things as age, social status, ethnicity, etc., there is a greater likelihood that they will quickly evolve similar attitudes toward the way their roles and responsibilities on the board should be carried out.

4. In some boards, there are members with disproportionately larger resources (largest checkbooks, influential friends, political connections, etc.) who have a greater amount of influence in the group. It is not that they intentionally manipulate others, but nonetheless they may have a larger voice than others in shaping board culture.

5. One of the strongest influences shaping board culture is the behavior of those in the critical leadership positions of Board Chair and CEO. While these positions do not have formal authority to make board decisions, they do carry a great deal of informal influence over the process.

6. Finally, in addition to the influence of the Board Chair/CEO positions, some boards evolve small sub-groups within themselves, sometimes referred to as cliques or "core groups" (Bradshaw, Murray, & Wolpin, 1992). These informal groups are not recognized officially in any way though they may dominate certain committees or formal offices. They are important because the attitudes and beliefs of their members regarding how the board should operate or what position it should take on various issues can significantly impact those who are not part of the group. It is important to realize that "core groups" are not necessarily a bad thing. Sometimes they emerge simply because some people have more time and interest in the organization so do more and find others with a similar outlook to whom they naturally gravitate. Other inner groups develop because they are made up of people with similar periods of long tenure on the board (part of the founder's syndrome phenomenon discussed earlier). This is especially common when there are no fixed maximum terms of office for board members. New members might come and go but a core of "old timers" stays around.

   Core groups become a problem when they engage in any of the following behaviors:
   - Control of information or a willful disregard for providing proper orientation to new members thus leading them to feel like outsiders;
   - Pushing an "agenda" of their own based on interests or positions on important issues that may not be shared by others; and
   - Engaging in "backstage" politicking in the form of "secret" informal meetings outside of regular board meetings to plan how to have their positions on issues approved at the meeting.

However, whether or not core groups are a positive or negative influence on the board, it is useful to recognize they may exist and discuss the role they play so everything is out in the open.

Treatment

Changing a board's culture can be very difficult because, by definition, it is something that has developed over time about which many are not consciously aware. So the first step in the change process must be that of surfacing what has heretofore been taken for granted. How to do this?

- One way is through the use of fully confidential self-assessment exercises such as the Board Check-Up, University at Albany, SUNY sponsored research project offered online for free by www.boardcheckup.com. This questionnaire, which includes the items above, is especially useful if effort is made to obtain accurate, anonymous perceptions of the board's culture from board and non-board people who have occasion to observe and/or interact with the board. When results show, for example, that some respondents perceive that there is an inner group that has more influence than others, this finding needs to be put before the whole board for discussion. This discussion should cover the following points:
  - What is the evidence that suggests such a group exists?
  - If there is consensus that it does, why has it emerged?
  - Most importantly, is the behavior of this group good for the board or not-so-good? That is, on balance, do the group's actions contribute to, or reduce the effectiveness of the board's decisions and/or individual members in meeting duties of their fiduciary role?

  The objective of this open discussion of the perception of an inner group on the board is not necessarily to do away with it. Indeed the board might well want to encourage it since they often do more than others are able to do. Instead, the goal is to work on ways to keep them open and communicating with all board members and discourage "backstage" maneuvering. One of the best ways to prevent negative sub-groups from developing is to conduct regular exercises in team building for the board. The more the board as a whole thinks of itself as a team, the more sub-groups within it are likely to be positive, open and sharing.

- In a similar way, the use of outside consultants may yield insights into the workings of the board that the board has been unable to see for itself.
- One advantage to having, and enforcing, by-laws that specify fixed terms of office for board members is that there will always be new members joining at regular intervals. Usually new members are expected to adopt social norms or go along with the ways of operating the board has followed in the past. However, if a conscious effort is made to ask new board members to provide critical feedback on their perceptions of how the board is working, a surfacing process might take place and needed changes in board culture might be made. However, if a board does engage new members in a change process, it must be open to new information and careful not to be critical of those who are honestly trying to share their perceptions in a constructive way.

- Finally, it is difficult to over emphasize the importance of the Board Chair and the organization's CEO in creating and changing the unspoken culture of the board. Their leadership styles often set the tone for the way in which the board exercises its collective leadership of the organization. To learn more about the competencies of highly effective chairs, boards, CEOs, and leadership volunteers, see the next chapter on leadership.

To learn more about culture in nonprofit boards and organizations and how to influence it see the websites in Table 10.

Table 10

Additional Board Culture Resources

Topic	Country	Source Website
Organizational Culture: General	U.S.A.	Free Management Library http://managementhelp.org/organizations/culture.htm
		The Bridgespan Group http://www.bridgespan.org/Publications-and-Tools/Organizational-Effectiveness/Four-Actions-Nonprofit-Leaders-Can-Take-to-Transfo.aspx#.U27DE4FdX84
		http://www.bridgespan.org/Publications-and-Tools/Leadership-Effectiveness/Lead-and-Manage-Well/Strategies-for-Changing-Organizations-Culture.aspx#.U27Ny4FdX84
	Britain	KnowHow NonProfit http://knowhownonprofit.org/organisation/orgdev/structure-and-culture/culture
		http://knowhownonprofit.org/leadership/change/organisation/copy_of_culture
Board Ethics	Australia	Australian Institute of Company Directors http://www.companydirectors.com.au/Director-Resource-Centre/Not-for-profit/Good-Governance-Principles-and-Guidance-for-NFP-Organisations/Principle-9-Culture-and-Ethics
Team Building in Boards	Australia	TMS Worldwide http://www.tms.com.au/tms12-3c.html

Chapter 10

Leadership on the Board

Symptoms

Most literature on the leadership function of nonprofit organization boards concentrates on the role of the board *as a whole*. This emphasis is because, legally speaking, it is the final authority for the organization—even though it may delegate some of its authority to a CEO. Similarly, it recognizes that no one board member may legally act as a representative of the entire board on a given matter unless given authority to do so by the Board itself.

Just as in other work groups, however, boards have both formal and informal individual leaders within them—people who have a significant influence over how the group works and how effective it is. For example, as previously discussed, some boards develop influential core groups within them and they can be a positive or negative force for change

While these kinds of informal leaders and groups are important to identify, it is generally agreed that the most influential leaders in nonprofit organizations are the board chair and the CEO. In many small voluntary organizations with no paid staff, the board chair and CEO may be the same person (though it should be noted that it is illegal for charities in some jurisdictions such as New York, to have Chair/CEO leadership roles held by the same person).

A high percentage of agreement with the following statements might indicate problems with leadership of the board:

☐ There is a kind of "inner group" that seems to run things on the board and those who are not part of it sometimes feel left out.

☐ The board chair tends to be overly controlling.

☐ The board chair seems to have her/his own "agenda," which is not always shared by others.

☐ The board chair is a bit too passive and/or disorganized in her/his leadership style.

☐ The board chair's meeting leadership skills are not as strong as they could be.

☐ As far as I know, the board chair is reluctant to speak to board members who don't carry out their responsibilities properly.

☐ As far as I know, the relationship between the CEO and the board chair is quite formal; they don't talk much "off the record."

☐ As far as I know the CEO rarely consults individual board members for informal advice or assistance.

☐ There seems to be a lack of trust between the CEO and the board.

☐ The information that the CEO provides the board to help it make decisions is sometimes inadequate or too slanted.

☐ The CEO seems to be trying to dominate or control the board too much.

Diagnosis

It is important to realize when respondents check the statements dealing with leadership that they are providing their perceptions only, not an "objective" reality. Also, it must be remembered that the reasons people are perceived as being more or less effective leaders may, or may not, lie within the leaders themselves. In other words, it is possible that situations and circumstances may create conditions that make it difficult for almost anyone in a leadership position to be perceived as effective. It is also possible that a person in such a position might be very effective under one set of circumstances but not in another. The case of Winston Churchill is often presented as the most vivid example of this—a universally acclaimed leader during WWII who was defeated in the polls once peace was restored after the war. Times changed and he was no longer seen as the leader people wanted.

With respect to reasons for perceptions of leader ineffectiveness, our research suggests there are five major ones:

1. Lack of role clarity. In our research on board chairs, we found a significant positive relationship between clarity of key actor roles and perception of chair leadership effectiveness.

2. Situational factors. For example, in our research, we found evidence of a negative relationship between CEO turnover and perception of chair leadership effectiveness and impact. This finding suggests that stability in CEO tenure may be associated with being seen to be effective.

3. The board's own prior ineffectiveness—its failure to adopt "good governance practices" is associated with perceptions of poor leadership. Our research and that of others (e.g., Ostrower, 2007) points to a significant positive relationship between the reported use of good governance practices (e.g., strategic planning, board performance assessment, assessment of CEO leadership and organizational effectiveness, etc.), and perceived leadership effectiveness. Because all of this research was based on one-point-in-time correlational methodologies, however, it is not possible to say whether the presence of good governance practices makes it more likely that leaders will be seen as effective, or whether leaders who are seen as effective are more likely to use their influence to help their boards adopt good governance practices.

4. The personality traits leaders bring to their position. In our research it was found that chairs who were perceived as being honest, humble and helpful were also more

likely to be seen as having more impact on the performance of the board, the CEO and the organization. The same relationship was found between perceived chair effectiveness and perceptions of chair's "emotional intelligence" (i.e., as someone who is self-aware and able to manage others in relationships) and in possession of the traits associated with team leadership (being open, fair, respectful, able to create a safe climate where issues can be discussed, one who recognizes others, and does not distract them from goals, etc.). The findings of this research are supported by general leadership studies that show leader personality to be a strong influence on leader effectiveness (see Miller & Droge, 1996).

5. The involvement of followers with leaders. Our research on board chairs found that when members of a group spend more time with the leader and have more interaction with her/him, they are more likely to see the leader as effective. This could be due to the nature of the role they play. (For example, the CEO, board officers and committee chairs are more likely to interact frequently with the Chair than "ordinary" board members, staff or external stakeholders). This explanation assumes that the "closer" people get to their leaders, the more likely they are to think favorably of them. These results suggest that leaders will benefit from spending time building high quality relationships with others.

Whatever the reason, leadership ineffectiveness can be costly for the board and organization that fails to address it. Cost can be seen in board and CEO turnover, level of engagement, job dissatisfaction, low social cohesion, poor board morale, lack of public trust, inability to innovate, etc. For a full discussion of the informal leadership that may be exerted by "core groups" within the board, see Chapter 8 on Board Culture.

Treatment

The results obtained from this section of the Board Check-Up are the most sensitive and potentially difficult to handle of any. Most people, when asked if they would like to have their job performance reviewed, tend to say they welcome feedback on how they are doing so they can use it to improve. In practice, however, many do not appreciate being what they see as "unfairly criticized" no matter how much effort is made to make it "constructive" criticism. Varying degrees of defensiveness and hostility are common reactions even though they may not be made obvious at the time. In one early experience with the Board Performance Self-Assessment instrument, for example, an instance arose in which a third of respondents indicated that they thought the board chair had difficulties running effective meetings. The board chair said nothing at the time but within a month quietly resigned, well before her term was up. One might argue that this was all for the best but this overlooks the possibility that, if these results had been handled differently, she might have reacted differently and, for example, obtained some training in meeting leadership.

The following are suggestions for dealing with perceptions of leadership issues:

- It is best if, before the results of the survey are revealed to anyone, the Survey Coordinator hold a discussion with both the CEO and the Chair about a hypothetical situation in which some board members report perceptions that these leaders are engaged in one or more of the problematic situations described in this section of the survey. This discussion should cover to whom these results should be communicated and how they should be interpreted.

- It is recommended that, at first, results should be communicated only to the person involved, e.g., the Chair or the CEO. It should also be agreed that there are various possible reasons for such results as described above, which should be explored and that they do not necessarily mean that the board is dissatisfied with the leader. It could be that there is a situation that the board needs to address that negatively impacts the leadership of the chair or CEO.
- Finally, it should be understood that all the behaviors described in this section could be addressed through additional training and/or coaching. It is quite possible that a different style of leadership is new to many leaders. Also, it is not always possible for Chairs or CEOs to find the time or opportunity to take leadership development courses. What is more possible, in many cases, is to find effective experienced leaders of boards who are willing to act as mentors or coaches to the Chair or CEO for short periods of time. Retaking the Board Check-Up after a period of such coaching can provide useful indicators of the extent to which leadership from these critical officers has improved and to what extent agreed upon goals have been reached.

Leadership Development

The preceding discussion addresses how to help key leaders such as the Board Chair and CEO develop their leadership competency but it does not get into detail about what these competencies should be. There is not the space here to get into this very large and complex topic, however, a few key points can be made. Perhaps the most important is that there is no "one best way" to lead in all situations. Different mixes of board member personalities and different external conditions call for differing approaches to leading. The key question the board should consider is *how can nonprofit leadership be managed for higher board performance?*

The majority of the items in the list of board leadership issues above relate to the leadership competencies of effective chairs and CEOs. Other items relate to leadership influence and impact. For example, our research has shown that board chairs seen as exerting too little or too much influence in the role are also seen as having limited impact on the board, the CEO, the organization, and the support of external stakeholders.

This research identified the following behaviors of highly effective chairs. Organized in clusters, they are:

- Motivation and style (e.g., is helpful, has a sense of humor, is empowering, friendly and humble).
- Capacity to lead (e.g., is committed to the organization, devoted in terms of time given to it, capable of seeing the big picture, able to handle contentious issues, and collaborative).
- Personal attributes (e.g., is bright/intelligent, trustworthy, confident, thoughtful, organized, focused, and creative).
- Ability to relate(e.g., is flexible, easy going, non-judgmental and calm).
- Ability to advance the organization externally. (e.g., possesses connections and influence with key people and is willing to use them (see Harrison & Murray, 2012; Harrison, Murray, & Cornforth, 2013).

Herman and Heimovics (2005) identified the following competencies of "board centered" CEOs. They are:

- Facilitate interaction in board relationships;

- Show consideration and respect toward board members;
- Envision change and innovation for the organization with the board;
- Provide useful and helpful information for the board; and
- Promote board accomplishments and productivity.

The National Learning Initiative (2003) also identified competencies of effective leadership volunteers saying they:

- Are motivated to serve (e.g., recruited for the right reasons, empowered for the service of mission/others)
- Create, shared vision, and align strategically (e.g., are informed, consider best practices, contribute to the development of. and commitment to. a shared vision that provides meaning and direction)
- Develop effective relationships (e.g., nurture a healthy organization and work environment, are socially aware and maintain effective relationships)
- Create value (e.g., open to innovation, creativity, and change; translate theories into action; are responsive and accountable)

One of the better ways to design the kind of leadership that is best for your organization is that offered by the Competing Values Approach to leadership effectiveness (see Quinn et al., *Becoming a Master Manager: A Competing Values Approach*, 5th edition, for a description of the leadership competencies, and assessment tools that can be used to assess leadership effectiveness). The Competing Values Approach to assessing and developing leadership competency recognizes there are different values that underlie leadership styles (e.g., the tendency to focus on people, strategic goals, management processes, innovation and changes in the external environment etc.) and that these values can create tensions between leaders involved in the governance process. They have created a set of diagnostic criteria to assess leadership effectiveness and surface tensions in the leadership process. To develop leadership, they say leaders simply need enough information to adjust their behavior rather than to alter it altogether. This "balanced" approach to leadership development, which recognizes there are competing values and leadership styles, should reduce tensions and the tendency for organizations to swing from one ineffective leader to another.

Regardless of the approach or tool used, leadership development is an opportunity for nonprofit boards to:

- Assess leadership competency and isolate the contributions nonprofit leaders make to the board and organization through the governance process.
- Discuss tensions that exist between leaders and groups in the governance process. Nonprofit leaders should also discuss how to develop leadership competency and overcome situations in cases where leadership effectiveness is challenged (e.g., crisis, board chair or CEO turnover, etc.).
- Develop a focused plan for nonprofit leadership development that will be reviewed as part of the board performance assessment process.
- Increase responsibility of leaders in the governance process (e.g., from board member with no committee responsibilities, to committee member, officer and ultimately, chair of the board).
- Recognize leaders for their leadership contributions to the board and organization.

Table 11 contains additional useful information and resources to increase the governance effectiveness of the organization through leadership.

Table 11

Additional Board Leadership Resources

Topic	Country	Source Website
Leadership Development: General	U.S.A.	National Council of Nonporofits http://www.councilofnonprofits.org/resources/resources-topic/leadership
		The Bridgespan Group http://www.bridgespan.org/Publications-and-Tools/Career-Professional-Development/DevelopMyself/How-to-Develop-Yourself-Nonprofit-Leader.aspx#.U27eO4FdX84
	Canada	Ivey Business School, Western University http://iveybusinessjournal.com/topics/leadership/profiling-the-non-profit-leader-of-tomorrow#.U27f34FdX85
Leadership Assessment Tools	U.S.A.	Board Source https://www.boardsource.org/eweb/asae/default.html
CEO Leadership Development	U.S.A.	Stanford Social Innovation Review http://www.ssireview.org/articles/entry/the_leadership_deficit
	Britain	KnowHow NonProfit http://knowhownonprofit.org/leadership/role/chiefexecutive/framework

Chapter 11

Conclusion

The purpose of this guidebook has been to a) help you understand some of the issues that challenge the effectiveness of nonprofit boards, b) offer some explanations as to why they exist, and c) provide guidance on how to manage them so as to improve the effectiveness of the governance function.

The book, and the Board Check-Up research project of which it is a part, is derived from the idea of health checkups in medicine. The social science that underlies the research is that of the theory of organizational change. Simply put, by surfacing issues (symptoms) in the governance process, the stage is set for potential change in governance practices (treatment). However, as anyone involved in nonprofit organizations and governance knows, making change is easier said than done. In fact, our early research results that track the impact of Board Check-Up show that, while the majority of boards do report making changes in governance practices in each of the dimensions assessed in the Board Check-Up not all boards do so and some kinds of changes are made more often than others (e.g., issues related to board meetings are made more frequent than changes in board culture and leadership) (see Harrison and Murray, forthcoming). For this reason, we recommend boards take the Board Check-Up on a regular basis and use it as an opportunity to delve deeper into discussions of the symptoms and why they exist in the board (diagnoses), and what can be done about them (treatment). Results from our research of the change process show the Board Check-Up fills gaps in board leadership and technical capacity to self-assess performance (Harrison, 2014).

In addition to providing a model, theory and online tool for deciding change, we've also provided links to additional resources that may be useful when deciding what practices need to change. While resources are organized by country, many provide useful guidance and tools that apply across countries. By no means do we provide an exhaustive review of the websites and literature on governance effectiveness in this book. Please consider additional sources and adopt those that seem to be a good fit for your board and organization.

Where Do You Go from Here?

The final section of these Guidelines is directed primarily at those who are using them to self-assess board performance as part of an organization registered to take the Board Check-Up at www.boardcheckup.com or who are part of a course on nonprofit governance of which the Board Check-Up is a learning activity. It describes ways in which the results of the Board Check-Up can be used to promote dialogue and decisions regarding needed changes in governance practices.

The results of the Board Check-Up will give you some ideas about possible difficulties that could be keeping your board from performing at its best. How these results are used will determine how valuable they might be in helping to make changes that will make the governance function of your organization more effective. Here are some suggestions for getting the most from the self-assessment process.

1. As a general rule, it is desirable to take action on the results of the questionnaire as quickly as possible after it is completed, while the process is still fresh in everyone's minds. If possible, create a small "Board Self-Assessment Implementation Task Force" to take the lead in this final phase. Alternatively, an existing board committee such as a Governance or Executive Committee could take on this job.

2. This committee should choose a chair—possibly the person who acted as Board Check-Up Coordinator.

3. It should review the findings and discuss the best way to present them to the board as a whole.

4. A special board meeting, or retreat, should be organized to review the findings. If possible, all those who were originally asked to participate should be invited, e.g., in addition to board members, ask top managers, senior volunteers, etc.

5. The special board meeting or retreat should proceed as follows:

   A. The Chair of the meeting should begin by reviewing the reasons for engaging in this self-assessment exercise and go on to make the following points:
   - The discussion should *not* take the form of blaming anyone for any of the issues identified.
   - It is possible that some problems, on further discussion, will be found to be simply the result of lack of knowledge or experience on the part of some participants. These can be corrected by better communications.
   - When there *is* a strong consensus that certain issues are real problems it is important not to jump to conclusions about why they exist or what should be done about them. Instead, they should be carefully analyzed. We therefore recommend that this special board meeting *not* be used to make decisions but only to seek consensus on issues and identify possible solutions. The Task Force would promise to take this input and return later with well-thought-out formal recommendations for change, if needed.

   B. Discuss the significance of the results obtained in each of the topic areas covered in this Final Report.
   - Response rate
   - Percentage of "Not Sure"
   - Total score
   - The 10 things we do best
   - The 10 issues that might be the most challenging
   - Results for each of the nine distinct elements of board effectiveness

   C. If the group is large enough, consider breaking into smaller groups to discuss the following questions, otherwise pose them in a plenary format:
   - What are the issues that most need working on in terms of importance and immediacy?

- For each of the top priority issues, why do they exist? (The meeting should be reminded that the reasons might not always be simple. For example, if there is strong agreement that board meetings are too long, this could be for many reasons: a failure to establish and enforce time limits for agenda items, board members being unprepared, poorly prepared committee reports, too much time spent on routine leaving important policy issues until late in the meeting, etc.)
  - What positive, future-oriented changes might be made to end the problems?

6. The Implementation Task Force should take the input provided at the special board meeting and use it to prepare a series of recommendations for change along with supporting arguments for them. These would be brought to a formal meeting of the board for discussion and approval.

7. Finally, responsibility for tracking the outcomes of these changes should be allocated to a person or committee who will report at the end of a year on the degree of improvement in the governance process. This should signal the beginning of a process of board self-evaluation that occurs every year.

Continuing and long-lasting effectiveness in governance practices are best achieved if the board commits itself to assessing its performance on a regular and long-term basis. Here are three options for you follow to ensure this kind of long term success:

1. Be part of cutting-edge research

This guidebook is part of a larger research study of nonprofit board effectiveness. Participants gain access to free online tools and resources produced from the research on the state of nonprofit board effectiveness in nonprofit organizations around the world. If you have taken the Board Check-Up online (www.boardcheckup.com), then you are a participant in this research. If you haven't, then consider registering for the University at Albany, SUNY sponsored research project online through the website or contact Professor Yvonne Harrison yharrison@albany.edu for more information.

2. Take an interactive nonprofit governance course for free or credit

In January 2015, Professor Harrison opens her University at Albany, SUNY Nonprofit Governance course to the public as part of the Open SUNY strategy to increase access to education through online learning. Coursera's online teaching platform hosts the course and interactive instructional strategies are incorporated to teach course concepts, which include main concepts in this and other nonprofit governance books. Through the course learning activities, participants receive guided instruction on board performance assessment. Along with faculty and specialized educational technology support, peer learning groups support and evaluate teaching and learning in the online environment.

3. Join a peer learning group to develop and help grow your board and the field of nonprofit leadership

Participants in the Board Check-Up research and Nonprofit Governance course will be invited to join various nonprofit leadership peer learning groups on topics of importance to participants. These groups will be facilitated by faculty, nonprofit leaders, and students in the University at Albany and SUNY Open community.

References

Aulgur, J. (2013). *Nonprofit Board Members Self-Perception in the Role of Organizational Governance and The Balanced Scorecard*, Dissertation. Retrieved online from: The University of Arkansas http://gateway.proquest.com/openurl?url_ver=Z39.88-2004&res_dat=xri:pqdiss&rft_val_fmt=info:ofi/fmt:kev:mtx:dissertation&rft_dat=xri:pqdiss:3588504

Bradshaw, P., Murray, V. & Wolpin, J. (1992). Do nonprofit boards make a difference? An exploration among board structure, process and effectiveness. *Nonprofit and Voluntary Sector Quarterly*, *21*(3), 227-249.

Bradshaw, P., Fredette, C. & Sukornyk, L. (2009). *A Call to Action: Diversity on Canadian Not-for-Profit Boards*. Retrieved from http://www.yorku.ca/mediar/special/diversityreportjune2009.pdf

Brown, W. (2007). Board performance practices and competent board members: Implications for practice. *Nonprofit Management and Leadership, 17*(3), 301-317.

Brudney, J. and Murray, V. (1998). Do intentional efforts really make boards work? *Nonprofit Management and Leadership, 8*, 333-348.

Brudney, J. and Nobbie, P. (2002). Training the policy governance model in nonprofit boards. *Nonprofit Management and Leadership, 12*(4), 387-408.

Cameron, Kim. (n.d.) *The Competing Values Framework: An Introduction*. Retrieved from http://competingvalues.com/competingvalues.com/wp-content/uploads/2009/07/The-Competing-Values-Framework-An-Introduction.pdf

Carver, J. (2006). *Boards that make a difference*. San Francisco: John Wiley & Sons.

Chait, R. P., Ryan, W. P., & Taylor, B. E. (2005). *Governance as leadership: Reframing the work of nonprofit boards*. New Jersey: John Wiley and Sons.

Cornforth, C. J. (2001). What makes boards effective? An examination of the relationships between board inputs, structures, processes, and effectiveness in nonprofit organizations. *Corporate Governance: an International Review, 9*(3), 217-227.

Fredette, C. and Bradshaw, P. (2012). Social capital and nonprofit governance effectiveness, *Nonprofit Management and Leadership, 22*(4), 391-409.

Gill, M. (2005). *Governing for results: A Directors guide to good governance*. Mississauga, Canada: Trafford.

Green, J. C. & D. W. Griesinger. (1996). Board performance and organizational effectiveness in nonprofit social services organizations. *Nonprofit Management and Leadership, 6*(4): 381-402.

Harrison, Y.D. (2014). What influences changes in governance behavior and practices? Results from a longitudinal study of the effects of online board performance assessment on nonprofit governance effectiveness, Paper presented at the annual conference of the Association for Research in Nonprofit Organizations and Voluntary Action (ARNOVA), November 20, 2014, Denver, CO.

Harrison, Y. D. (2014). Optimizing the potential of Information and Communications Technology in nonprofit organizations. In K. Seel (Ed.), *The management of nonprofit and charitable organizations* (pp. 465-516). Toronto: LexisNexis.

Harrison, Y. D. & Murray, V. (2012). Perspectives on the role and impact of chairs of nonprofit organization boards of directors: A grounded theory mixed-method study. *Nonprofit Management and Leadership*, *22*(4), 411-438.

Harrison, Y., Murray, V., & Cornforth, C. (2013). The role and impact of chairs of nonprofit boards. In C. Cornforth & W. Brown (Eds.), *New perspectives on nonprofit governance.* Routledge, UK.

Herman, R.D., & Renz, D.O. (1998). Nonprofit organizational effectiveness: Contrasts between especially effective and less effective organizations. *Nonprofit Management and Leadership*, 9, 23-38.

Herman, R.D. & Renz, D.O. (1999). Theses on nonprofit organizational effectiveness. *Nonprofit and Voluntary Sector Quarterly*, *28*, 107-126.

Herman, R., & Renz, D. (2008). Advancing nonprofit organizational effectiveness research and theory. *Nonprofit Management and Leadership 18*(4), 399-415.

Herman, R., Renz, D. O., & Heimovics, R. D. (1997). Board practices and board effectiveness in local nonprofit organizations. *Nonprofit Management and Leadership*, *7*, 373– 385.

Herman, R. & Heimovics, D. (2005). Executive leadership. In D. Renz (Ed.), *Jossey Bass handbook on nonprofit management and leadership.* San Francisco: Jossey-Bass.

Hodge, M.M. & Piccolo, R. F. (2011). Nonprofit board effectiveness, private philanthropy, and financial vulnerability. *Public Administration Quarterly*, *35*(4), 520-550.

Holland, T.P. & Jackson, D.K. (1998). Strengthening board performance: Findings and lessons from demonstration projects. *Nonprofit Management and Leadership*, *9*, 121-134.

Jackson, P. (2006). *Nonprofit risk management and contingency planning.* Hoboken, New Jersey: John Wiley and Sons.

Kaplan, D. & Norton, D. (1996). The Balanced Score Card: Translating Strategy into Action, Boston: Harvard University Press

Kooiman, J. (2003). *Governing as governance.* London: Sage.

Millesen, J. (2004). Sherpa? Shepherd? Conductor? Circus Master? Board Chair. *The Nonprofit Quarterly*, 39-42.

Miller, C. (2008). Truth or consequences: The implications of financial decisions. *Nonprofit Quarterly*. Retrieved from http://quarterly288.rssing.com/browser.php?indx=14322835&item=43

Miller, D. & Droge, C. (1986). Psychological and traditional determinants of structure. *Administrative Science Quarterly*, *31*, 531-560.

Murray (2010). Chapter Title. In D. Renz (Ed.), *Jossey Bass handbook on nonprofit management and leadership.* San Francisco: Jossey-Bass.

Murray, V. (2014). Managing the governance function: Developing effective boards of directors. In K. Seel (Ed.), *The management of nonprofit and charitable organizations in Canada.* Toronto: LexisNexis.

National Learning Initiative (2003). What do voluntary sector leaders do? A report on a Joint Project of The Coalition of National Voluntary Organizations and The Association of Canadian Community Colleges. Retrieved from http://www.vsi-isbc.org/eng/hr/pdf/nli_report.pdf

Ostrower, F. (2007). Nonprofit Governance in the United States. Center on Nonprofits and Philanthropy, The Urban Institute.

Quinn, R. & Rohrbaugh, J. A. (1981). A competing values approach to organizational effectiveness. *Public Productivity Review*, 122.

Quinn, R. E. & Rohrbaugh, J. (1983). A spatial model of effectiveness criteria: Toward a competing values approach to organizational analysis. *Management Science*, *29*, 363 377.

Quinn, R. Faerman, S. Thompson, M. McGrath, & St. Clair, L. (2010). *Becoming a master manager*. San Francisco: John Wiley and Sons.

Renz, David O. (2006). "Reframing Governance." *Nonprofit Quarterly*, *13*(4), 6-13.

Renz, David O. (2012). "Reframing Governance II." *Nonprofit Quarterly*, Special Governance Issue, accessed online at https://nonprofitquarterly.org/governancevoice/21572-reframing-governance-2.html.

Tompkins, J. (2005). *Organization Theory and Public Management*, Belmont: Thomson Wadsworth Publishers.

Zaccaro, S. J. & Klimoski, R. J. (2001). *The Nature of Organizational Leadership*. San Francisco: Jossey Bass.